A SCHOOL FOR EACH STUDENT

Personalization In a Climate of High Expectations

Nelson Beaudoin

EYE ON EDUCATION
6 DEPOT WAYWEST, SUITE 106
LARCHMONT, NY 10538
(914) 833–0551
(914) 833–0761 fax
www.eyeoneducation.com

Library of Congress Cataloging-in-Publication Data

Beaudoin, Nelson.
  a school for each student: personalization in a climate of high expectations.
    p. cm.
  Includes bibliographical references and index.
  ISBN-13: 978-1-59667-079-2 (alk. paper)
  1. Individualized instruction. 2. Student-centered learning 3. Educational leadership. I. Title.
  LB1031.B415 2008
  371.39′4—dc22

                                                                2007051781

10 9 8 7 6 5 4 3 2 1

Production services provided by
Rick Soldin, Electronic Publishing Services, Inc.
Jonesborough, TN — www.epsinc-tn.com
Editor: Robbin Brent Whittington,
Asheville, North Carolina — www.rbrent.com

Dedication

To all those students who
sit in our classrooms yearning to
become relevant.

Meet the Author

With more than thirty-seven years of experiences in educational leadership, Nelson Beaudoin brings practical and exciting ideas to the discussion on school reform. His work is guided by the belief that leaders should listen more than talk, care more than judge, and understand more than guess. Beaudoin has led two high schools through a Comprehensive School Reform grant. His schools have received national recognition both as a Service Learning Leader School (2001) and as a First Amendment School (2004). He was selected Maine's 2000 NASSP Principal of the year. He has presented his message on inspirational leadership, the magic of student voice, and creating a culture of change throughout the country. His faculty's work on Professional Learning Communities, Student-Led Conferences, and Student Engagement has been replicated in numerous schools.

His first book, *Stepping Outside Your Comfort Zone: Lessons for School Leaders*, demonstrates that great things can happen when school leaders refuse to settle for business-as-usual. His second book, *Elevating Student Voice: How to Enhance Participation, Citizenship and Leadership*, shows schools how to empower students. This book explores factors that lead to greater student success, a success achieved by changing the focus of schools from "all" students to "each" student.

Beaudoin is currently the principal at Kennebunk High School in Kennebunk, Maine.

Contents

Preface

Writing a book intended to challenge current thought about how schools should be structured is a process that is both daunting and inspiring. Knowing that my ideas and opinions will be publicly scrutinized, perhaps inviting judgment from readers whose views might be very different, is a frightening proposition. However, that fear is countered by the heartening possibility that this book may create a more enriching learning environment for students. The promise that this work will allow educators to focus on each student and have a positive impact on schools makes this endeavor far more rewarding than risky.

As I labored through countless writing drafts, the idea of having school leaders incorporate these ideas into their own work provided ongoing inspiration. The vision of a principal asking teachers to read this book in order to create better outcomes for their students has guided and sustained my efforts. I believe strongly that administrators and teachers need to hear and consider the information presented in this book and that all schools could benefit from these ideas and beliefs.

Schools are, in many ways, places of common and transferable events and storylines. The anecdotes found in this book are factual accounts of events as they actually happened. It includes real stories and real strategies about real schools. I share them in order to provoke your thinking about education and to offer concrete ways to rethink current practices and programs. I wish to offer an alternative vision; one that will steer the conversations about educational improvement away from a one-size-fits-all approach to a personalized method that places each student in the center of the equation.

My desire to illuminate the tenets of great schooling has deep roots. I have been a student, teacher, or administrator in ten different high schools since entering ninth grade in September of 1963. Over the ensuing forty-five years, I have witnessed grand successes and disappointing failures in the institutions I have called home. In most cases, the difference between success and frustration was not due to some magical program or super human effort, but rather a clear alliance between educational beliefs and educational practices. While many people go into education because they want to help young people grow and achieve, sadly, most of our schools are structured to keep students powerless. This book will demonstrate the possibilities that abound for students, teachers, and schools when we are willing to start from a fundamental place where each student has value and a voice.

Although I concur with many who believe that the American education system is in crisis, I do not agree with the one-size-fits-all remedy that clutters the backdrop of school reform. What is needed most rarely becomes part of the solution. In order to begin working toward solutions, we must invest in ideas that work. We need to focus more on maximizing the performance of each student rather than comparing their accomplishments with those of other students. We need to recognize that expectations have a lot more to do with input rather than outcomes. We need to place a spotlight on the importance and promise of our students, instead of their limitations. By adopting personalized practices, we can inspire more of our students to work at a higher level and exemplify the adage that success breeds success.

We will explore attitudes and beliefs common to all educators and make the case that the answers to our most perplexing problems are found right in front of us: in the students we teach. A foundational shift in the fundamental mission of schools can provide us with much-needed progress. A distinct shift from a school for all students to a school for each student can lead to greatly improved learning outcomes by meeting the needs and desires of each student.

The "school for each student" model of reform is not unlike many other ideas currently being offered to improve schools in that great teachers and administrators are the delivery system. Any increase in the effectiveness of schools must start with you, the educator. You have picked up this book, so I will assume that you are receptive to the idea of improving the learning environment at your school. You may be curious about the prominence of the word EACH in the title. Or perhaps you have simply grown tired of the mandates of "No Child Left Behind" and are searching for a better direction. In either case, I encourage you to take this journey with an open mind and consider how closely these ideas will align with what you truly believe about your work with, and influence on, each student entrusted to your care.

You are embarking on a journey intended to compel you to look at your school, your work, and your students from a new perspective. Within each student lies the magic and promise needed for us to be more successful and fulfilled as educators by better meeting their needs. Our work, after all, is first and foremost about our students. I trust that you will find this undertaking to be well worth your time and effort. Change usually starts with one person, one idea, and one strategy at a time. The challenge of creating a school for each student starts with you!

How To Use This Book

This book has been written to help educators investigate their attitudes toward students, to consider the extent to which students should become the focus of educational programming, and to improve learning outcomes for every student. On one level, this book has been structured to create a couple hours of personal introspection that will expose readers to the straightforward idea of creating a school for each student. In that sense, I can see a fairly traditional interaction between the reader and the material presented. The ideas brought forward are given consideration within the context of the reader's experiences and invoke agreement, disagreement, action, or inaction. Any changes in teaching or administrative practice will occur based on the individual reader's willingness to consider and implement these ideas. If you are one of those who wants a quick read that focuses on truly teaching students rather than improving test scores, then welcome! I hope you feel enriched and inspired by reading this book.

On another level, this book was designed to lead educators into conversations about relevant issues facing education today. One of the central themes in this book is the idea that educational outcomes improve in a climate of reflection and collaboration. This work is intended to provide groups of educators with professional discussion topics that will prime conversations about school reform. It was written with the hope that the material presented could be embellished through text-based conversations. Whether this book is used with a reading partner, in a book group, or as part of a team or full faculty professional development activity, the outcomes based on widening the perspective of participants can be exponential.

The book is divided into six chapters, each with a specific focus that is introduced in a brief section overview. Following the overview is a series of short sections that expand on the chapter topic. Each section can be read in less than five minutes, while the longest chapter can be read in about a half an hour. This format allows for immediate reflection upon, and discussion about, the ideas presented in each section at group meetings. Finally, at the end of each chapter you will find discussion questions for the preceding material. These questions are designed to help readers reflect back on the material throughout the entire chapter and to consider the relationship among the topics.

If you wish to utilize this book as part of a professional development activity, the following suggestions are designed to guide your journey. How you utilize each of these suggestions depends on the structure of your book study. The list below is intended to provide you with a few ideas:

Small Group Study

1. Approach the material using a traditional book group format. Each participant reads assigned segments of the text and the group gathers to discuss.
2. All participants read the chapter overview and each participant is responsible for reading and sharing assigned sections within the chapter with the rest of the group.

Large Group Study

1. Divide into teams of 6–12 members with each small group following 1 or 2 above. After small group conversation, each group selects a spokesperson to represent their group in a fish bowl discussion.
2. Conduct a text-based seminar to be held in a fish bowl. All participants read the same material, and then a small number of participants discuss the reading in a facilitated seminar. Others listen actively with a vacant chair available for observers to join the conversation.

Introduction:
Why Don't We Get This?

I believe we know with certainty what works in schools. In fact, we can synthesize all the thoughts of our educational leaders and experts and come up with a fairly short list of effective teaching methods. Good education has never been a mystery. Bonnie Benard, in her research on resiliency, found three essential protective factors necessary to support the development of young people. She found that caring relationships, high expectations and providing students opportunities to participate and contribute are fundamental factors for youth success.[1] Each of these factors can be found in the circles appearing in Figure 1 below:

Figure 1 Protective factors in young people's environments

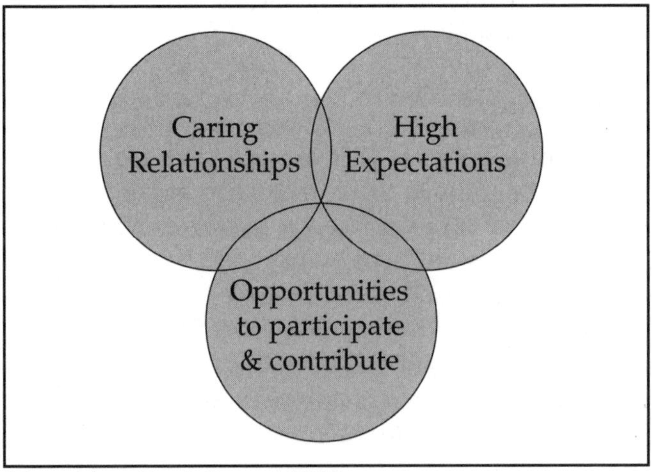

Caring Relationships

High Expectations

Opportunities to participate & contribute

Adapted from Bonnie Bernard (2004)

---

[1]Bonnie Benard (2004). *Resiliency: What We Have Learned.* West Ed.

Caring Relationships

Benard's findings are not a rarity; you can sift through the works of countless scholars and researchers and find startling commonalities. All the educational leaders that I site in this section speak of educational success in the context of three very similar areas of focus. What Benard calls a caring environment, Robert Evans terms nurturing,[2] and Michael Fullen refers to as personalization.[3] Bill and Melinda Gates chose forging relationships as their first of three "R's",[4] while Russell Quaglia, from the Global Institute for Student Aspirations, speaks of giving each student a sense of belonging and accomplishment.[5] In similar fashion, Alfie Kohn speaks of building a caring community as a key to creating a successful school.[6] We could continue by adding more names of educational visionaries and their corresponding terminology, but the point has been made. Many educational leaders advance an interpersonal idea to coincide with Benard's notion of caring relationships. Virtually every successful person I know was, at some point in their educational years, touched by the interpersonal aspects of teaching that are represented in the "Affective" column in Figure 2 on the following page. We can call it nurturing, caring, relationship building, personalization, or, as Steven Covey[7] would say, "loving," but most importantly we know that it is central to educational success.

The interpersonal side of education formulates one of the key elements of a school for each student, and ideas to advance emotional connections will be woven throughout this work. I will assert and offer support for my thesis that if we intend to accomplish great outcomes for our students, we first have to impact them emotionally.

---

[2]Evans. Robert. *Family Matters: How Schools can Cope With the Crisis in Childrearing.* Jossey-Bass Publishers, 2004.
[3]Fullen, Michael, Peter Hall, and Carmel Crevola. *Breakthrough.* Corwin Press, 2006.
[4]The Gates Foundation, www.gatesfoundation.org
[5]Quaglia, Russell. Quaglia Institute for Student Aspirations, www.qisa.org/about.php
[6]Kohn, Alfie. "The Risk of Rewards" *Teachers.net Gazette* 2, no. 4 (2001).
[7]Covey, Stephen. *The 8th Habit.* Simon and Schuster, 2004.

Figure 2 Essential components of successful schools

	Affective	Substance	About Them
Benard	Caring relationships	High expectations	Opportunities to contribute
Gates	Relationships	Rigor	Relevance
Quaglia	Sense of belonging	Challenge and motivation	Leadership and taking action
Evans	Nurturing	Structure	Latitude
Kohn	Caring community	Engaging curriculum	Student choice
Fullen	Personalization	Percision	
Covey	Love	Learn	Leave a legacy

High Expectations

The recent standards and accountability movement directs us toward the second circle on Benard's short list of what is vital for quality schools: high expectations. Again, using varying terms, they all say essentially the same thing. Benard calls for high expectations; Gates talks of rigor; Evans stresses the need for structure; Quaglia stresses challenge and motivation; Covey brings the forth the idea of learning; Michael Fullen promotes the thought of precision; and Kohn stresses the need for an engaging curriculum. They all refer to the standards or learning outcomes educators strive for. What is it that we are trying to get students to learn and be able to do? What is the substance of our work and how can we improve our practice to help our students get it? This book will consider these questions of how we can go about the work of improving teaching and learning, or the "Substance" column as seen in Figure 2, by adopting a mission that supports the success of each student. Within the context of putting teaching and learning in the forefront, rigor, structure, standards, and motivation will be included in the discussion; not so much what we should teach in terms subject specific content, but how putting students in the center of the process can be used to lead them to great achievement.

Throughout our examination of creating a school for each student; we will consider the idea that schools cannot improve unless we put great teachers in the classroom. Regardless of how invested we are in the other areas of importance in education, we cannot possibly reach our objectives without great teachers; who trump everything else in education. Here again, the idea that we already know the answer to the question about what quality teaching is will be highlighted as we explore what great teaching looks like in a personalized school setting. As much as this work is intended to challenge and aspire teachers to greater achievement, it is written knowing full well that many teachers labor painstakingly to accomplish great things in nearly impossible settings. I hope the focus on quality teaching will validate their work and encourage educational policymakers to provide them with the resources and support needed to achieve their mission.

Participation and Contribution

The third component for achieving successful academic outcomes is my favorite and, arguably, the one that gets the least attention. In her third circle, Benard challenges educators to not only hold young people to high expectations in a caring environment, but also to give them opportunities to participate and to make a contribution. The Gates Foundation similarly suggests that the third "R" should be to make learning relevant. Evans suggests that providing students with latitude is essential to their success, while Alfie Kohn advances of the importance of student choice. Quaglia proposes that students be given opportunities to lead and take action. All of these ideas are really about giving students a chance to make a difference, or what Covey refers to as "leaving a legacy." The belief that this slant on education belongs on our short list of what works in schools comprises a significant part of this book. The third column in Figure 2, "About Them," describes how educational leaders refer to this third component of quality schools.

We will continue to further develop the idea of students making a contribution and explore ways in which we can help accomplish this objective. You will see that when this is done well, it can become the underpinning of exceptional schooling. You will learn that, above all else, we must strive to help our students become relevant. The philosophy of, "helping students become relevant," has been at the heart of my work for nearly two decades. With each passing day, I become even more convinced that we must make an effort to help students become somebody, or, as Sam Chaltain—the former co-director of the First Amendment Schools Project and executive director of the Five Freedoms Project—says, "to make them visible."[8] Stated in another way, adults need "to teach," while students need "to be."

A chapter of this book will be devoted to each of these three necessary components of successful schools: caring relationships, teaching and learning, and helping students become relevant. A fourth chapter has also been included to look at leadership strategies, promoting change, and other ideas intended to widen educational perspectives and to help develop a culture in our schools that focuses more on each student.

While the ideas advanced in this book are deceptively simple and straightforward, the ideals they represent are vitally important. But this does not mean the tools needed to improve our schools are complicated or mysterious. Every resource we need resides within our own beliefs and attitudes about young people. School improvement and success for each student will only become possible in a climate of hopefulness and trust. Hopefulness and trust are cultivated in an environment that recognizes the power of effective education, the substance of what we are trying to accomplish with our students, and an unwavering commitment to make schools about them.

---

[8]Chaltain, Samuel, www.fivefreedoms.org

Chapter 1

It Is About Them

"The work of educators should be about
helping students become visible"[1]
—Sam Chaltain

The French documentary, *To Be and To Have*, provides us with a wonderful model for making education about each student. George Lopez, the celebrated teacher in a one-room schoolhouse in rural France, shows remarkable skill and ability to keep his focus on the students.[2] Each time I watch this documentary, I am amazed at how calmly Lopez approaches his responsibilities as a teacher. It is as if the world around him moves in slow motion. The educational and emotional needs of each student are always in the forefront of his vision, and all else seems secondary. In this moving tribute to teachers everywhere, Lopez personifies the ability to be patient, nurturing, organized, attentive, firm, caring, sensitive, and dedicated. Many of those skills will be highlighted in the sections that follow. As you explore the ideas presented in Chapter 1, hold this visual of a teacher giving unwavering attention to each student. Remember that our work is always about them.

---

[1]Chaltain, Samuel, www.fivefreedoms.org
[2]*To Be and To Have*. Nicolas Philbert. Video. New Yorker, 2004.

We begin our journey of how to create a school for each child with our first task of making our work as educators be about the students. At first glance, this should be the easiest idea of all to incorporate into our work, but, sadly, it is one of the hardest. I, and I suspect most teachers, went into education to be with kids and to help them learn. The notion that our work should be about the children should be a foregone conclusion, yet I am saddened to say that this is not the case. Our original purpose is diverted away from the students and instead becomes more focused on curriculum content, test scores, parental demands, financial issues, teacher comforts, the race to college, and political agendas. Educators are slaves to these demands, and, consequently, their primary attention to their students is often compromised.

As it stands, educators barely have time to focus their attention on students in a general way. Yet, we must pay attention not only to all students in a general sense, but to each student in a very concentrated, specific way. This is a huge challenge, but one well worth embracing.

The sections in this first chapter help to clarify various ways that giving attention to each student can be accomplished. Much of what will be presented falls in the category of beliefs and attitudes. If you think a certain way about students and your role as a teacher, then the ideas presented should pave a fairly smooth road toward implementation. I suspect, however, that the ideas presented will create tension for even the most student-centered reader. Attention to each student is a rarity in schools. Part of the challenge that you will face as you work toward a school for each student model is the institutionalized and established traditions that funnel your attention away from your students.

I contend that this unwavering attention to students is possible. I believe that when it is done well, the other demands on teachers and schools become more manageable. Rather than carving time away from our students to accomplish all of the peripheral responsibilities common to education, focused time with each student at the heart of our every action makes all those other responsibilities doable.

A School for Each Student

Many years ago, an ad campaign for the McDonald's restaurant chain used the slogan *"We do it all for you!"* to suggest that customers needn't worry about decisions when ordering food: *"Two all-beef patties, special sauce, lettuce, cheese, pickles, onions, on a sesame seed bun!"* In contrast, the Burger King franchise chose a different approach: *"Hold the pickles, hold the lettuce, special orders don't upset us!"* Burger Kings slogan was *"Have it your way!"* (See Figure 3).

Any personal thoughts regarding the nutritional viability of fast-food restaurant aside, if the slogan "We do it all for you!" described a school, I think it would be "a school for all students," where students have a curriculum already chosen for them and little or no opportunity to make a contribution. At a school that says, "Have it your way," students would participate in a variety of personalized programs that honor their strengths and interests. This is "a school for each student," and I support this approach. Rather than trying to force all students to fit the same structure, we would encourage each student to find a structure that fits him or her. Rather than students following predetermined courses of study, they could pursue passions,

Figure 3 We have to keep reminding our kids that school is about them

Two all beef patties special sauce lettuce cheese pickles onions on a sesame seed bun!	Hold the pickles hold the lettuce special orders don't upset us!
We do it all for you!	Have it your way!

which can lead to adventurous learning. I do not view students as spectators who let education happen to them. Since school is about students, their participation is non-negotiable. The words of a Monte Selby song express this idea quite well.

> *"All students in reach when we find their rhythm*
> *The step, the dance, the song within them.*
> *That's a better journey, but so much harder.*
> *Too extraordinary, but so much smarter*
> *To drum to the beat of each different marcher."*[3]

While most schools would have all students march to the beat of the same drum, this book advocates a substantially different approach: drumming to the beat of each student. We will explore ways that teachers and administrators can move their schools and classrooms toward this idea of finding the beat of each different student. The topic, however, is substantially more complex than the simple analogies to fast food restaurants or marching to the beat of a drum. In the sections that follow, you will be provided with multiple ideas that can be incorporated in schools to advance personalization strategies for each student. These strategies and ideas will enable you to look at school reform and improvement through a different lens: a lens of possibility.

---

[3]"Beat of a Different Marcher." By: Monte Selby and Debbie Silver, Rec. ©℗ 2002, Street Singer Music, BMI and Tato Tunes, ASCAP. All right reserved. Used by permission.

The Magic Is in Them

I have been a long-time believer in the premise that education is really about helping students become themselves. We may teach skills and knowledge and we may do many other things for our students, but we are merely helping students to discover who they are. The following poem captures the essence of this idea.

WIZARD[4]

The kids walk in, stroll in, bounce in, flounce in, strut in,
dance in, and finally stagger into my classroom.
There are even a few who look and act like they have been
swept up by a tornado and dropped in the back row.

Each in his or her own way is following the yellow brick road
to my door in search of the Emerald City and the Wizard of Oz.
Some need courage and I support and believe in them
until they believe in themselves.

Some want a heart and I introduce them to art, music, theater,
and poetry and let them explore their feelings.
Some are in search of a brain and I help them locate theirs
and show them how to use it to the best of their ability.

Some are trying to find a home and I give them a safe,
secure place to be with an adult who listens and cares.
I am not really a wizard so I use my teaching skills to
help my students learn that the magic is within them, not me.

—Keith Harvie

As Harvie suggests, we need to use our teaching skills to help students understand that the magic is in them. I believe this idea is a tough sell for many educators because so many people who have chosen this profession have done so with the

---

[4]Harvie, Keith. "Wizard," *Maine Educator* 66, no. 8 (April 2006).

intent of doing great things *for* young people. To sustain their initial naive motivation to do great things *for* students, teachers will oftentimes view students as incapable, even though their intentions are good. Consequently, some educators are much more likely to rescue students than to facilitate opportunities for self-discovery. My own experiences as a father provide a perfect illustration of how adults can carry this concept of helping students too far. The account that follows demonstrates how some adults can unknowingly keep students from developing in order to justify the necessity of their role in the relationship.

I assume that my two sons were pretty typical growing up. They wanted to help me whenever I worked around the house—until they hit their teenage years. Reflecting back on those times, I am sad to say that I missed many opportunities to let them work alongside me. On occasion, I was too busy to involve them in projects, but more often than not my reluctance to let them help had to do with my shielding them from the burden of work I associated with adulthood. In my head, I thought a good father should be working to protect their childhood. So instead of having them help me rake leaves or pound nails, I would tell them to go play. When they did get to help pound nails, for example, I grew discouraged and frustrated as they struggled with the skill.

The next time I needed to do some hammering, I either would tell them that I did not need their help, or that the work was too hard. A number of unconstructive outcomes surfaced from this type of scenario. From an educational point of view, I did not give them the impression that they were capable. I did not hint that the magic was in them. I chose to do things for them rather than let them experience the setbacks and challenges associated with hard work and learning. Teachers need to guard against this type of enabling. My role as a dad should have been to patiently work alongside my sons and encourage their gradual acquisition of skills. Luckily, I got to spend a great deal of quality time with my boys, but it was mostly about play, not work. Fortunately, they got the opportunity to develop their work ethic through athletic and artistic pursuits, so they overcame the liability I had unknowingly created for them.

Looking back, I realize that I missed some great opportunities to spend time working with my sons and they missed opportunities to acquire some important life-skills. Back then, I certainly did not have the idea of helping them become relevant on the agenda.

This chapter of the book focuses on what schools could and should do to involve students in the educational process. In order to embrace the discussion that follows, you must first shed the idea that students are incapable. This journey will take you away from the idea that teaching is about doing great things *for* students and bring you to the realization that it is about helping students do great things for themselves. It will take you beyond the ordinary conversation about student participation to a place that recognizes that the magic is within each student. Please repeat after me, "The magic is in them, not me!"

Learning by Doing

I frequently tell the story of a seventh-grade girl who shared a wonderful metaphor for letting students learn by doing. Several years ago at a Service Learning conference, I participated on a panel that included a 12-year-old girl named Tina. During one session, a room full of educators and community leaders asked panel members various questions about service learning. One person asked the panel what role adult leaders should play in service learning programs that had a strong focus on students as planners. As the adults on the panel stumbled through less-than-inspiring responses, Tina waited for a chance to speak.

Once she finally got the floor, Tina explained that the adult role was to keep students safe while allowing them to learn by doing. She suggested that the role of educators was to act as "bumpers" on a bowling lane in order to keep the ball from going into the gutter while still giving even the youngest of bowlers an opportunity to experience the game. Tina's metaphor provides a great example of the role of a teacher who wants his or her students to learn by doing rather than doing it for them.

The implications for educational practice are far-reaching. Learning by doing gets at two important considerations for our students. First and foremost, it provides relevance to the activity they are engaged in and at the same time holds the promise of providing students with a sense of accomplishment. Rather than approaching a particular skill or activity theoretically, students can view it practically. Rather than imagining the purpose of acquired knowledge, they actually get to apply it in a real-world setting. The concept of keeping kids safe as they learn by doing extends far beyond service learning programs.

Using the skill of writing as an example, it would be pretty simple to provide students with copy after copy of good writing and ask them to work at replicating what they see. It may be harder, but arguably so much more effective, to have students work through the writing process as an exercise of growth and discovery. Students become great writers by doing, not by emulating. This brief example of writing, although vulnerable to attacks by writing teachers who might cringe at my uncomplicated suggestion, really represents a paradox for teachers. Are we trying to get all students to write like Emerson, or are we trying to cultivate the world's next great writer? Or is it both?

There is probably not a correct answer to this question, but it is clear to me that educational policy-makers are hovering very close to a cliff edge when they put more emphasis on outcomes—such as test scores—than they do on the processes that encourage students to learn by doing. Instead, the journey to a particular learning outcome is what we should treasure.

Similarly, teachers are approaching that edge if they see their jobs as getting students to know what they know and travel the same route to learning that they themselves traveled. We can spend hours trying to conclude what Shakespeare intended with each of his soliloquies, or we can spend hours discussing what each soliloquy invokes in our students. I prefer the latter. Learning must be an expedition that students embark on for themselves, with teachers serving as scouts and guides. Shakespeare's intentions may be helpful in the learning process, but students need to be guaranteed the opportunity to experience learning by doing.

I am reminded of Tina's metaphor about the bumpers on a bowling lane each time I see a student come alive because of some intellectual discovery. That excitement and sense of accomplishment generates more enthusiasm for learning and provides fuel that leads to the next discovery. Youngsters are so excited when they knock down pins at the bowling alley. Thank God for the bumpers, and thank God for teachers who allow students the opportunity to learn by doing.

Start Small

Earlier, I told how I rarely let my sons work with me because I mistakenly wanted to shield them from the realities of hard work. However, we did experience some exceptions to this pattern of parenting that may provide some useful examples of how the smallest of opportunities to help, provided by teachers or adults, can lead to young people feeling relevant.

My wife and I were building a house when our oldest son, Jamie, was eleven and our younger son, Matthew, was seven. During that intense time of construction and hard work, there were some great memories of how my sons found ways to become involved. Early in the process, Jamie was watching me lay out the location of exterior studs on the foundation plate. I was using a framing square to mark the location of each stud 16 inches on center. At one point, he asked me why I was flipping the framing square over each time I marked the location of a stud. He suggested that all I had to do was slide the square down the board until I was against the previous mark and the edge of the framing square would give me the next 16" mark. He was right, and his new process was quicker and provided less opportunity for errors. I let him mark the location of studs from then on and, to this day, I remember how proud he was of this accomplishment. He had helped me improve. In that instance, he had become the teacher.

On another occasion, Matt helped me put together an intricate box beam that I had designed to span a vast area over our kitchen so we could avoid having to put in a supporting post in the middle of the space. The box beam was made up of an outer skin of plywood nailed and glued to 2-by-4 studs. The box beam design allowed for more strength and load-carrying capacity than a regular beam. The design called for a very close nailing pattern with nails two inches apart along the whole 24-foot length of the beam and up and down the 30-inch beam at 12-inch intervals. Matt was up for the challenge of driving in all these nails. He would experiment with different techniques to make the job go quicker, but he mostly just diligently worked until the beam was complete. At one point he figured out how he could drive two nails in at one time along the seams of the plywood. Upon completion, I know that he felt he had made a significant contribution to our building project and also felt proud of the discovery of what he felt was a time-saving technique. It did not matter that his technique actually took more time; he would figure that out on his own as he gained more experience. After all was said and done, he had driven in every nail in the box beam; it was a small accomplishment in terms of building an entire house, but a huge accomplishment in the eyes of a seven-year-old. It mattered little that I had struck chalk lines all along the beam to show him exactly where he should place each nail. In essence, I had provided him a learning aid, similar to bumpers on a bowling lane.

Several months later, as I was preparing to install asphalt shingles on the roof of our home, I hurt my back. Roofing is backbreaking work, even for a healthy person, but we had to find a way keep moving forward with the construction project. Lugging shingles up a ladder to the roof was a task that took all of my strength when I was in good health. With a bad back it was impossible. My wife, Sharon, and our two boys ended up breaking the bundles of shingles into fourths and developed a relay system up an interior stairway and through a second floor window to get the shingles up to the roof so I could apply them. We were able to shingle our entire roof without hiring outside help because we broke the task down into manageable chunks for our young boys. They were about to help and feel good about their valuable contribution.

In schools, students do not have to perform monumental feats to feel a sense of importance. Many years ago, one of my teachers started an "America Reads" model at our high school, and the sense of importance of even the smallest acts of achievement were unmistakably evident. High-school students left study hall, loaded onto a bus, and rode to the nearby elementary school to read to their first grade buddies. With very limited training and an investment of a relatively small amount of time, these teenagers made a fantastic impact. The first-graders saw them as heroes, and this definitely contributed to the high school students' sense of importance. Each contribution we allow students to make creates a positive situation for them and becomes the foundation for even larger contributions.

Several years later, students at the same high school became involved in a program aimed at teaching foreign languages in fifth-grade classrooms in our district. This foreign language program required much higher levels of training and a greater time commitment than the "America Reads" program. However, the outcomes for both the younger students and the older students were similarly magnificent. We can start small and build steadily as youngsters gain confidence and experience.

Making a Contribution

At the end of the day, young people (in fact, all people) want to feel like they have made a difference. This is a basic human need; the need to feel like we are making a contribution. Even the youngest of students want to be part of something important. Given all the problems facing us, whether in a personal, community, or global context, wouldn't it make sense for us to accept all the help we can get, regardless of who is providing it? I always find it astonishing when adults attempt to exclude young people from the opportunity and the joy of making a difference. Young people can be such magnificent assets to their communities and do not need to be sentenced to silence and invisibility as they await adulthood.

To illustrate this, let me share a story about a young man named Ryan Hreljac. At the age of six, Ryan heard a speaker in his first-grade classroom talk about the lack of clean drinking water in parts of Africa. He learned that without clean water, people could become ill and even die. He also heard that for a mere $70 a well could be drilled that would provide people in that region hope for a healthier life. Ryan went home and shared his learning with his parents and shared his plan that he intended to raise $70 to pay for a well. He asked his parents to give him chores to do so that he could earn money. He started bringing out the trash, washing dishes, sweeping the garage, and helping mom and dad however he could. In four weeks, the determined Ryan earned the $70 and proudly accompanied his mother to the agency to present his gift. Unfortunately, he was told that he had misunderstood and that the cost of a well was $1000, not $70. Ryan was unshaken by the development. He looked up at his mom and heroically said, "I guess I need to do more chores!"

Years have past, but now Ryan, through the Ryan's Well Foundation,[5] has raised over $1,000,000 to bring clean drinking water to people in Africa. What started out as a 6–year-old boy's dream to help others has become an important charitable foundation.

---

[5]Ryan's Well Foundation, www.ryanswellfoundation.org

Schools are full of boys and girls like Ryan. Young people who are excited about making a contribution to their community or their world. We, as educators, must find ways to tap into that compassion and harness that energy. That is why service-learning and community service experiences can be so meaningful. Doing meaningful service activities in the community helps students feel relevant.

If academic learning can become part of the package, as in service-learning, than not only does the student achieve relevance, but the learning itself becomes relevant. In my experiences, service-learning has two important components that distinguish it from community service. One is that the students are involved in planning what they are going to do for service, and the second is that the service connects to the students' academic learning. When both student ownership and academic learning occur, student outcomes become richer.

In schools where I have seen service-learning programs take hold, student benefits have been remarkable. Schools at all grade levels have discovered that there are many places where students can make a contribution. Service-learning can take many forms, but among the most common strands are intergenerational, humanitarian, civic, and environmental. Although these four strands are somewhat self-explanatory, I have included a few representative projects from each.

Intergenerational

- A high-school environmental science class writes and performs a play about conversation for district fourth graders.
- High-school eleventh-graders interview World War II veterans and write their stories, culminating the project with a luncheon tribute to the greatest generation at a local retirement complex.
- Sixth-graders run workshops for senior citizens on the use of e-mail and internet.

Humanitarian

- A high-school English class studies modern-day slavery and organizes a school awareness assembly along with a fund-raiser in order to earn enough money to free a slave.

- A primary school's physical education students learn about the benefits of exercise and living tobacco-free while raising money for the American Heart Association by doing a "Jump Rope for Heart" project. In turn, they earn points towards purchasing physical education equipment for their school.
- A middle-school social studies class adopts pen pals from a school in Mexico and organizes a drive to send them badly needed school supplies.

Environmental

- A high-school science class classifies, plants, and maintains the necessary vegetation to sustain a wetland as part of a school building project.
- A middle-school science class develops and manages a school-wide recycling program.
- A student energy team is created in a school to publicize and oversee conservation practices in the school.

Civic

- A high-school government class develops a system to register citizens to vote.
- An eleventh-grade social-studies class researches the impact of a proposed piece of legislation and presents their findings to a state senate subcommittee.
- A middle school history class helps identify and document gravesites in a cemetery that dates back to the Civil War.

All of these examples, and hundreds more like them, show the wide range of projects that classroom teachers and schools can explore to develop rich learning experiences for their pupils. Students want to be part of something important, and schools can tap into the passion to make a contribution through service-learning.

Similarly, schools can invoke strong feelings of accomplishment in their students by promoting community service opportunities. Programs like "we care" projects that occur through a school's advisory program can get students involved as contributors. This elevates their sense of accomplishment. Whether students decide to support a "coats for kids" campaign, raise money for hurricane victims, or support a local family that lost their home in a flood, the results lead to students feeling relevant.

I have heard much criticism about how education is often too theoretical and not practical enough. Schools can do more to bring the world into the school and vice versa. Given how easy it is to tap into our young people's need to feel important, there is no excuse for schools making students feel irrelevant. We need to make sure we are not stifling any student's desire to make a contribution to their school or community, because in that desire lies a key to greater student participation and involvement.

Getting Students To Care

A student came to see me several weeks before our planned September 18, 2006, activity fair at Kennebunk High School. This student wanted permission to start a new club at our school. She was interested in starting an Independent Women's Club as an outgrowth of a column she had written for a local newspaper. It would be aimed at informing our female students about pertinent issues facing teenage girls, such as relationship violence, peer pressure, and body image. At this particular time, there were several other clubs and activities being added to our rich list of student activities. I had requests to support a grill team (a cooking club that would provide food at some of our smaller athletic events), an Anomie club, a guitar club, a Frisbee club, a yoga club, a running club, and a video-gaming club. All of these ideas for student activities were supportable.

The Independent Women's Club, however, was more than just a fun, high-interest activity like grilling or playing a guitar. It was an organization that had a higher purpose and a mission of contributing to the greater good.

I approved all the clubs, but none as quickly and as passionately as the Independent Women's Club. It would be important to know that the student who made this proposal was not a mainstream student leader as you might suspect. The student was a bright, but seemingly disenfranchised, student at our school. She was a bit counter-culture, dressed the part, and resisted stereotypical high-school activities. Her involvement in this new club changed all of that. She became a real leader in our school. The activity fair yielded a high level of student interest in the Independent Women's Club and the organization attracted multiple sign-ups. Within weeks, this student was back in my office getting permission to send a small contingent of high school girls to a conference on teen issues offered by a county agency called Caring Unlimited. She also made a proposal to collect used cell phones from students and staff to benefit a state-wide domestic violence prevention program. I approved both requests, and the ripple effect of one student having a passionate idea touched many others within the walls of our school and beyond.

Five months into the clubs existence, ten shivering members were featured in a picture on the front page of a local newspaper as they proudly took part in an Atlantic Plunge to raise money for women who are victims of abuse.

This spring, an English teacher shared with me a copy of a journal entry one of her students had written while visiting Ireland. As the student was comparing the differences between the school she was visiting in Ireland and Kennebunk High School, she referenced a wild conversation she had participated in with her Irish hosts. She created quite a stir while explaining to the classroom she was visiting about her involvement in the Independent Women's Club back home. These words concluded of her journal entry:

> *"It wasn't until that day that I realized how lucky I am to be part of this group, especially seeing it was started by students. In their school, there are only clubs that the teachers make up. They don't have a say in what they want to do. So many girls all over the world would be so interested in a group like ours, and it makes me ashamed that 99% of them will never get an opportunity like this which they deserve."*

The Independent Women's Club, in their first year of existence, asked for permission to plan and implement a workshop for middle-school girls to help them with the transition to ninth grade. They also proposed that I send a contingent of four students to a state-level women's issues conference so they could learn more. I approved enthusiastically and wondered how many other young girls in our state would have this opportunity for personal growth.

The student founder of our Independent Women's Club was not only making a wonderful contribution to her school and community, but I also believe she was making a wonderful contribution to her own development. She learned how to lead, to take action, and, most importantly, she learned that passion is an engine that drives social change. She, in effect, became a better student. She now has a higher purpose for attending class, learning skills, and connecting to others. Facilitating all of this is, or should be, part of every educator's mission statement. Our work should be about getting students to care.

All of the interest in student clubs and activities at our school provides a stark contrast to Robert Putnam's book, *Bowling Alone: The Collapse and Revival of American Community*. Throughout his book, Putnam makes the case that membership in social organizations which prospered in the mid 20th century had dramatically dropped off as the century drew to a close. I theorize that working towards getting student to care has the potential to reverse these social trends. That has certainly been the case at my school. Clubs have doubled in number over a six year period and membership in most activities continues to soar. We have a situation where kids are eager to make a contribution because they know that their skills are valued. Most importantly all of these opportunities helps them to care about their school and their activities.

Chapter 1: Discussion Questions

1. How does the innate desire that educators have to contribute to the growth and success of young people sometimes hamper learning outcomes for students?
2. Do you believe that personalization enhances student learning? If so, how would convince others of its importance?
3. How would a classroom teacher (or a school) go about showing students that the are capable of making real contributions to their community. . . . now?
4. What is your reaction to the statement that we should work to create students who feel more like "volunteers" than "prisoners" in their school?
5. What do you currently do to make the subject you teach more relevant to your students' lives?
6. Generate a list of ways that your school could promote student relevance through meaningful participation in service learning or community service? What are the resources beyond the walls of the school that could assist you?

Chapter 2

Opportunities for Voice

"To me, a silent school is not a school at all."[1]
—Dennis Littky

Giving students a say in how their classrooms are structured is often referred to as student-centered instruction. My work in schools, particularly in the last decade, has focused on increasing student voices. This emphasis on a student's voice, I contend, increases their participation, leadership, and citizenship. I have come to believe that increasing students' voice in schools can have a dramatic affect on their achievement. Not only can teachers provide students with opportunities to have a voice in the classroom, but also school governance can be structured to provide students a real say in decisions that affect them. Much of what follows in this chapter deals with the school-wide implementation of programs to encourage student input. In the next section, we will outline a very specific program that a school might consider when striving to increase student participation. The table (Figure 4) below lists activities

---

[1]Dennis, Littky, Samantha Grabelle (2004). *The Big Picture: Education is Everyone's Business.* Association for Supervision and Curriculum Development.

Figure 4: The foundations of student voice

• Student Council	• Advisory Programs
• Class Officers	• Student-Led Conferences
• Co-curricular Activities	• Experirntial Learning
• Athletic Programs	• Student Exhibitions
• School Clubs	• Service Learning
• Student Publications	• Student Direct Programs
• Student Committees	• Student giving Teachers Feedback
• Student Speakers	
• Displaying Student Work	• Student on Hiring Committees
• Showcasing Students	• Student on School Board
• Community Service	• Student Centered Classrooms
• Student Surveys	

and programs that can be created in schools to offer students broad opportunities to utilize their voices and make a contribution to their schools.

The column on the left lists programs that exist in most schools, while the items in the right-hand column are less common. Obviously, most schools have athletic teams and school publications that allow students the opportunity to exercise their voices. Schools that provide opportunities for students to serve on school committees or include students on hiring committees are less common.

Of course, the degree in which these programs are actually student-led and student-centered could vary greatly from school to school. A student newspaper, for example, can be good or bad depending on exactly how free students are to use their own ideas. Much of the impetus for creating student-run journalism programs really comes from the need to have young people practice and understand the 1st Amendment—freedom of the press—that exists in our nation. Student voice is not just some frivolous refinement that schools should embrace; it is a necessity to train students for life in a democratic society. If students do not learn these skills in school, where else will they be able to get them? We need to give students the skills necessary to exercise their rights to free press, speech, religious beliefs, assembly, and petition.

Thomas Jefferson wrote:

*"I know of no safe depository of the ultimate powers of society
but the people themselves; and if we think they are not
enlightened enough to exercise their control with a wholesome
discretion, the remedy is not to take it from them but to inform
their discretion by education".*[2]

I suspect that most high-school graduates and a fair amount
of our nation's teaching force would be hard-pressed to accurately articulate what Jefferson was trying to say. In essence,
schools have not been living up to the vision that our founding
fathers had for preparing young people to live free. If the great
experiment in democracy is to survive and thrive, we must
structure our schools to provide students experiences in being
citizens of a free society.

In a proposal to develop "The Five Freedoms Network," a
school reform initiative, Sam Chaltain writes: "One of the great
paradoxes of human beings is that we feel two pressing needs at
the same time- the freedom that comes from defining ourselves as
individuals, and the security that comes from feeling connected
to one another. Sometimes, this paradox leads us to satisfy one
need at the expense of the other." Chaltain concludes however,
"that these two impulses are not mutually exclusive." One can
join a community without discarding their freedom and one can
be a strong individual without sacrificing their connections to
others. This is at the heart of what teachers and schools need
to do for students. Chaltain states: "Schools must be places that
nurture our need for individual freedoms as a means for forging
stronger collective bonds, and environments that create unity in
the interest of our diversity, instead of at the expense of it."

A by-product of student voice is the reality that combining
voice and choice results in empowerment, and empowerment
leads to strong feelings of ownership. I contend that involving
students in decisions that affect them will not only serve them
in their future lives, but creates a better school in the present.
In schools where student voice is an important consideration,
there is little debate about the positive climate that is created

---

[2]Jefferson, Thomas. Letter to William Charles Jarvis, 28 September 1820; *The
Writings of Memorial Edition*, eds., Lipscomb and Bergh, 15:278.

when adults seek out and honor the opinions of students. When schools involve students as part of the solution to organizational concerns, they move away from adversarial relationships and more toward cooperative ones. The graph below (Figure 5) tracks the student perception of school improvement that has occurred because of their voices at Kennebunk High School over the past five years. In February of 2002, after several months of a school wide focus on raising student voice, fifty percent of our students felt that student involvement was making a difference in their school. As the graph shows, that percentage has steadily increased in each subsequent year.

When 89% of our student body responded positively to a question like this one, it provided convincing evidence that opportunities for school improvement through student involvement are flourishing. These results provide an eloquent answer to the question of whether or not schools can create rich opportunities for students to raise their voices and contribute to the school community through active citizenship.

Returning to the earlier story about of our student newspaper, it is important to more fully understand the far-reaching impact of a quality student voice activity. In some schools, student publications are not well-received. They are either so sterilized that the student body has no interest in them, or so controversial that

Figure 5: Students have a voice in this school and I have seen changes occur because of student involvement.

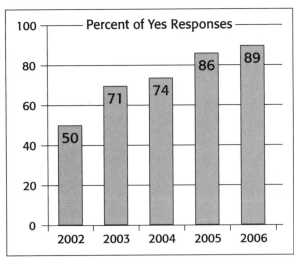

school officials cannot support them. At Kennebunk High School we, at least for now, appear to have it right.

When the newspaper, *Ramblings*, hits the hallways of our school, you can barely find a student's face that isn't buried in it. Based on the work of a great faculty advisor and a four-year run of excellent student staffers, our school newspaper is a mainstream activity in our school. Students line up to get on the newspaper staff as opposed to what happens at some other schools where newspapers are school-controlled, uninteresting, or published underground. When the assertion is made that student voice enhances student participation, citizenship, and leadership, one needs to look only as far as our school newspaper for compelling evidence. Following are two examples of what I believe demonstrates an effective platform to honor the student perspective that our school newspaper has achieved.

1. Drinking at School Dances

The faculty newspaper advisor informed me that the student staffers had conducted a student survey about people attending the homecoming dance under the influence of alcohol. The modest survey showed that 40 of the 44 people polled had known at least one person who had been drinking prior to arriving at the dance. The advisor anticipated that the newspaper staff was going to discuss including the results in their next issue and asked if I would want to join in the discussion. As you might imagine, printing this statistic in a widely circulated student newspaper would probably have quite an impact on my work as the principal of the school, so I decided to attend their next meeting.

A half-hour discussion took place about the pros and cons of printing the results. They talked about the validity of the information, the repercussions of printing it, and listened to my perspectives on the subject. I knew going into the meeting that I had no intention of telling the students that they could not print this information, but I also knew that if it was printed and taken literally, I would be in for some rough days responding to community concerns. Some students wanted to print the article to expose the fact that there was a drinking problem among the youth in our community, while others were fearful that we would shut down future dances based on the results of this poll. As the discussion went back and forth, the advisor pointed to a quote on the wall by Jack Fuller: "Responsible journalism seeks to accurately reflect important and interesting information in a timely fashion, doing no harm unless the social good achieved out-balances the harm." As Fuller's quote implied, the discussion switched from the topic of drinking at dances to the social responsibility of the newspaper staff. Before I left the room, I stated that there was no way that I would even think of asking them not to print this. However, I did caution them to carefully and thoroughly think through the issue.

A week later, the paper came out with a boxed-in graph showing that 40 of the 44 people polled personally knew someone who was drunk at the homecoming dance. Adjacent to the graph was the following disclaimer:

> The RAMPAGE would like to address the validity of this poll. There are over 800 students at this school. We asked a total of 44. While the results of this poll may appear overwhelming, you must keep in mind the percentage of people polled. Although we believe this information to be accurate, we acknowledge that data is subject to human error. More extensive research would have to be done for this to be a definitive statement. We at the RAMPAGE do not want this to be accepted as a definitive statement, but as a thought-provoking topic for debate.

The story ends with the newspaper printing a pretty edgy piece of information, but printing it in a way that was socially responsible. In the days and weeks that followed, there were some conversations about students drinking prior to coming to school dances, but the graph did not incite an over-reaction, which might have occurred if it had not included a disclaimer. By the same token, had the information been banned we would have had some major problems in the areas of censorship and covering up an issue that needed to be discussed.

2. Free Speech

The cover article of the April 12, 2007, issue of our newspaper was entitled, "Free speech case makes it to the Supreme Court." The article talked about the landmark free-speech case, *Bong Hits 4 Jesus*, that had begun five years earlier.

There was a political cartoon on the front page showing two students holding a banner that read "Bong Hits 4 Jesus." The article was very well-written and did a great job explaining free speech in schools and previous Supreme Court rulings. The article also included thoughtful responses about the case from student interviews. I heard no negative reactions to this appearing in our paper, yet in 2002 in Juneau, Alaska, the banner caused such a commotion that the controversy went all the way to the Supreme Court. Our newspaper article was our students reporting news that was pertinent to them in a responsible way. The cartoon did not get included for shock value; it was used to advance our school's understanding of free speech. Similar to the previous example, these types of articles make our paper relevant to our students. It helps them understand the value and the responsibilities of the freedoms we have. Schools have at their disposal multiple ways to encourage, provide, and cultivate student voice. Realizing that quality student-voice programs lead to greater student involvement and achievement should inspire the adoption of a similar program in your school.

Raising Student Voice
and Participation:
The RSVP Model

In the spring of 2006, Rocco Marano paid a visit to Kennebunk High School. As Director of Student Activities for the National Association of Secondary School Principals (NASSP) and the National Association of Student Councils (NASC), he had expressed an interest in seeing the work we were doing with student voice. His visit coincided with a program that we were rolling out intended to introduce the formation of a school senate. We hoped the program would help to explain our student-voice initiative for all students and give them the particulars of the First Amendment grant at our school.

We had trained a dozen senior students to work in teams of two or three and present a scripted program to all of our underclass students through social studies classes. The program took about 45 minutes in each class and concluded with a survey that asked students identify some of the major areas of our school that needed improvement. During these presentations, our senior facilitators utilized skits, handouts, and class discussion to address the following questions:

1. What is this thing called student voice?
2. What does the proposed new governance structure at our school look like?
3. How can individual students get involved?
4. How does the First Amendment grant affect us?
5. What ideas can students generate about improving our school?

Mr. Marano sat in on three of these presentations and later spoke of how impressed he was with what he saw. One class was particularly engaged and yielded rich discussion and high levels of student interest. Another class was a bit less participatory, while a third seemed very quiet but attentive to the senior leaders. In all cases, he saw the students at our school getting a very consistent message about the value of student input and involvement. In effect, he saw the best and the worst of our school's attempt to kick-start our newly proposed K.H.S. Senate program to accent our student-voice and First Amendment programs. He left our school impressed with our efforts to increase student involvement in the inner-workings of our high school and later contacted me about the idea of becoming personally involved in a national program that he and his colleagues were promoting. They wanted to revitalize student council programs to help improve student participation and contributions in schools throughout the country. In May of 2007, one of my students and I attended a national training in Washington D.C. In the fall of 2007, we will be involved in training a number of Maine high schools on the RSVP program.

On the following pages, you will find a synopsis of the RSVP model. This is a very structured program—available to all schools—to be utilized to begin moving a school toward the ideas being advanced in this book. This summary comes from the school implementation guide published by the National Association of Secondary School Principals.

> *Raising Student Voice and Participation (RSVP) is a student engagement program sponsored by the National Association of Student Councils (NASC) and the National Association of Secondary School Principals (NASSP). The RSVP process uses democratic dialogue to give students a chance to speak out and take action on issues in their schools and communities that are important to them. RSVP bridges the gap between the way schools function now and the way they might if students' input was taken into more serious consideration.*
>
> *At its core, RSVP asks students what they care about, what proposals they have for school and community improvement, and what actions can be taken, in cooperation with adults, to implement their ideas for positive change.*
>
> *In RSVP, student council leaders plan and facilitate a series of student summits that engage the entire student body in dialogues and assemble student action teams to carry out plans for resolving concerns identified in the summits.*
>
> *Easily integrated into existing student council programs, RSVP can be used by any NASC member school to develop*

practical civic skills and incorporate student voice in a structured way into school planning and decision making.

By participating in this program, your school is at the forefront of a national effort to engage students in their learning and encourage the active citizenship of young people.

The RSVP program is anchored in the vision and beliefs of the National Association of Student Councils.

It also supports the NASSP report Breaking Ranks II: Strategies for Leading High School Reform *by providing principals with a way to utilize the leadership of their student councils. RSVP reinforces the concept that student council serves as a practicum for civic education, giving all students the opportunity to apply democratic principles to learn more about governance of their schools and communities. Following the preparation outlined in this manual, students trained to run the RSVP program in their schools will use NASC-identified leadership skills necessary to successfully facilitate student summits and manage civic action initiatives.*

One objective of RSVP is to create the mind set and recognition that the student council is the school's primary vehicle for student voice and meaningful involvement. That it is through student-led initiatives that students are able to identify needs and address concerns in effective and productive ways, founded in educational values and supported by the principal and faculty members.

Student leaders, advisors, principals, and other participating school members can integrate RSVP into their student council agendas, train other student leaders to plan and facilitate summits, and involve others in the development and implementation of the activities that result in response to issues brought up in the summits.

The RSVP program gives student council leaders the training and resources to:

- *Reach out and engage all student populations in civic based activities that support educational curricula*
- *Facilitate summits that identify significant issues that students wish to address through dialogue, problem solving, and civic action*

- *Extend opportunities for leadership and involvement to non-elected students on student council-led initiatives*
- *Establish a process and framework for developing and implementing student-led action projects to address issues*
- *Assist principals in identifying and recruiting nonelected students to serve on various school committees.*[3]

You are encouraged to contact your state's Student Council Association for more information on how to become involved in, or implement, this program. It provides an established program that can be used to jump-start student voice in your school. You can choose to create your own model, as we did at Kennebunk High School in 2006 prior to Mr. Marano's visit, or rely on the collective expertise of the many schools involved in a national program such as RSVP. The primary objective is to give your students opportunities to use their voices and participate in the workings of their school.

---

[3]Printed with permission of the National Association of Secondary School Principals

Voice In the Classroom

In the previous two sections, a case was made for creating a school-wide culture to honor the voices and contributions of students. If these democratic ideals stop at the classroom door the effect of this program will be marginalized. If we truly are going to create laboratories of democracy and convince students of their relevance, this must be extended into the classroom environment. In her book, *The Democratic Differentiated Classroom*, Sheryn Waterman does a meticulous job of bringing educational models together and making a compelling case for classroom teachers to provide democratic opportunities for their students.

Waterman explains that the democratic differentiated classroom "is about teachers working beside students to hear their views and desires about learning, and then to help them translate those views and desires into valuable skills, knowledge and attitudes". The idea that students need to learn and practice personal decision-making about their education is at the heart of Waterman's work. The idea of giving students freedom, without creating disorder, is a challenge that all educators should embrace.

Differentiation, at least in experiences I have had with two different high-school faculties, evokes suspicion among already over-stretched teachers. The concept calls for more individualization than some teachers feel capable of giving- but I believe a lack of understanding creates these misgivings.

Several years ago, one of our Communities of Practice groups focused on differentiated instruction and actually provided our faculty with a remarkably simplistic definition. The spokesperson for the group indicated that if we knew our students, knew our content, and knew our strategies, then we were well on our way to differentiating. In essence, these three areas of knowledge—student, subject, and strategies—would create accessible and motivating learning for each student.

Waterman contends that when you add the component of student choice you are better able to meet individual needs. This all ties in with the idea that choice and voice lead to empowerment and creates a higher level of participation, involvement, and achievement opportunities for the student. The greater buy-in from the students and the increased personalization that is created by their self-advocacy makes the initial challenge of implementing differentiation less daunting. Once underway, classroom routines quickly become more manageable because the learner is in partnership with the teacher and students assume greater responsibility for the process.

If we strive to work with each student in a personal way, if we can involve them deeply in the process, and if they eventually develop skills of self-advocacy and responsibility, we are getting the job done.

I strongly suggest that you reflect on your work and determine how close you might be to adopting a more student-centered approach. I would also recommend that you contact an existing program, such as RSVP, to explore the possibilities of bringing a well-established program into your classroom and school.

Returning to Keith Harvie's poem, "Wizard" (p. 5), we need to remember that the magic lies within each student. I believe that no matter how teacher-directed you currently are, there are small steps you can take to move toward a more personalized, student-led format. It could be as simple as having students help in the development of classroom rules, or as complex as having students plan how they are going to help structure a classroom unit to ensure that it will meet pre-determined learning goals. Any steps that you take to thoughtfully engage students in planning their own work and learning experiences provides them with the practice they need to become self-directed, enthusiastic, life-long learners. The feelings of empowerment that are generated once students are given some autonomy in the classroom actually become a strong, self-perpetuating motivator.

Best of all, there are models out there that you can adapt to your unique situation. There is a teacher in every school who has a knack for creating student-centered activities. If you want to explore what teaching can be like when students pull on the same end of the rope as the teacher, examples are not hard to find. Sheryn Waterman's book would be a great beginning guide to help you create a more democratic classroom. As your interest peaks, you will discover that many of your colleagues have learned to trust that students can make responsible decisions and have adapted their practices accordingly. On the pages that follow, I have included a few scenarios to provide you with some examples of how others have created student voice opportunities in their classrooms.

1. Student-Led Unit Planning

Waterman uses a process called "Student-Led Unit Planning" as a way to motivate students by giving them voice and choice. In this process, which is detailed in her book, *The Democratic Differentiated Classroom*, students vote on themes for the whole class to study.

After the class chooses the theme, the student who suggested the winning theme is responsible for doing a bulletin board about that theme. Then, students and teachers work together to determine how best to address it effectively, and the teacher plans challenging standards-based assessments and activities that will promote student learning. Students work individually or with a small group to determine a project that will show their answers to one or more of the essential questions generated by the theme. The teacher completes lesson plans based on the theme, and the students complete a "project proposal" that they present to the teacher in a conference. Then, the whole class determines a "consensus rubric" that will guide teacher evaluations and peer feedback for students' projects.

Finally, students present their projects and also participate in one or more teacher-planned culminating events or assessments. The completed unit is a beautiful blend of teacher-led and student-led learning activities that are highly engaging, educational, and motivational. These activities promote high levels of student buy-in and, not surprisingly, achievement. With this model, no one fails and students rarely disrupt the class.

2. Literary Cooperation

An English teacher decided to share novels with his students as a way of responding to a school-wide initiative dedicated to encouraging students to read every day. He started by going to the media center and found novel sets that were appropriate to his students' grade level and interests. The teacher selected several books and lined them up on a shelf in the classroom. Students were asked to examine the books, pick one that caught their interest, and then prepare a book talk to persuade their classmates to vote for their book. After students presented their book talks, the class voted on the top four novels to read as a class. The top vote-getter became the book that the class read. The positive outcome of this process was that every student in the class willingly read the selected book.

3. Student-Led Parent-Teacher Conferences

Nearly a decade ago, in 1998, the high school where I was working decided to explore the idea of doing student-led conferencing as opposed to the traditional parent-teacher conferences. Through this initiative, we discovered that one of the best ways to enrich the conversation with parents regarding school is to involve the students in the process. This proved to be a huge, welcome departure from the traditional parent-teacher conferences that occur at school. Rather than have the teachers and parents discuss the students' progress and achievement, we asked the students to plan and lead the conversation. The student involvement personalizes the process, helps students learn to advocate for themselves and articulate how they work and learn. If there are deficiencies in the student's approach to learning, they are present to help strategize solutions. Conversely, if there is cause for celebration because of their achievement, the students are present to reap the accolades.

Student-led conferences promote a higher level of accountability for the student even within a very basic format. When we first started these conferences, we were simply asking students to share with parents where they currently stood academically, where they were heading, and how they were planning on getting there. These straight-forward expectations yielded some incredibly complex and remarkable conference plans; students created formal exhibitions and built impressive portfolios. This method of conferencing is now very widespread and spans all grade levels. Even elementary age youngsters can have a voice in conferences and high school students clearly need this type of experience as they prepare for interviews by employers and college admission personnel.

4. Artful Peer Assessment

Providing student voice in the classroom does not require an intricate "out of the box" plan. It can be, and usually is, much less complicated. I recently observed a high-school sculpture class doing a peer critique of student-created wire sculptures. It was evident, from beginning to the end, that this unit was a haven for democratic experiences for the students involved. Early in the process, they had developed project expectations, timelines, and assessment rubrics. They had created parameters in terms of materials, size, accessories, and theme and had agreed on how each student would select a project. They were all to create a sculpture out of wire that represented a sporting activity that they were passionate about. The sculpture was to conform to a very clear self- and peer-generated assessment rubric that was clear, concise, and easy to apply and understand.

During the observation, the students presented their sculpture to their peers, responded to questions about their work, and heard critiques, both warm and cool, from the class. Interestingly, the teacher sat in the back of the room, doing nothing but beaming with pride at the quality of the students' work and the insightful critiques that other students were sharing. You can sometimes tell that you are in a great class by seeing who is doing most of the work, teacher or students. A simple yet powerful way to motivate students is to make the work their own instead of the teacher's.

All the work the students had done was inspiring, but I left even more amazed at how student-centered the class was. Students took responsibility for their learning outcomes and their finished works did not disappoint.

5. History Gets a Voice

The last example involves another relatively simple idea that a teacher developed to promote student voice in the classroom. This happens to be history class, and the project involves students writing letters to someone who has had an effect on history. At the end of the project, the students would write a letter to someone they chose and ask them questions about what it is like to affect history. The recipients of the letters would range from Presidents and Kings, to grandparents, to soldiers serving in foreign lands.

What made this project so outstanding was how the teacher walked each student through the process of how to select a person they would want to write to, and how he helped the students create their own question bank. This teacher, who had many years of successful teaching experience and who had spear-headed this assignment many times, could have simply done this for the kids, but rather he helped them create and discover questions for themselves. It was a wonderful moment when a dignitary responded to a 14-year olds question, and even better to know the student created the question. At the conclusion of the project, as responses started coming in from famous people or relative unknowns, excitement rippled throughout the school and community.

Waterman says, "Believing that this kind of classroom can work is half the battle; the other half is making it work."[4] It involves constant reflection on the question of whether or not you are really letting your students experience ownership in their learning process. If we conscientiously set out to become a more democratic teacher and work through the initial challenges that change invariably presents, we will be creating a more promising future for our students. We will be preparing them for the challenges of the full and engaging citizenship that awaits them in the real world.

---

[4]Waterman, Sheryn Spencer. *The Democratic Differentiated Classroom.* Eye on Education, 2007. p. 6

Democracy at Work

The process of empowering students and helping them prepare for the challenges of citizenship should not create a fear that students will take over the school or suddenly become revolutionists. I often hear that schools and educators are leery of some of the ideas presented thus far because of their fears, yet, in my experiences, I had to spend far more energy convincing students that they could actually use their voice than pulling in the reins of students who abused their freedom. The following story illustrates how student activism played out wonderfully at Kennebunk High School during the winter of 2007.

Three girls in the junior class made an appointment to see me, and my secretary, Karen, scheduled them for the last fifteen minutes of a school day. They entered my office promptly at the scheduled time. When I asked them what I could do for them, they began timidly, stating they had a problem with the school ring presentation that was scheduled to take place the following week. Further conversation revealed that these students discovered that the ring company was selling "dirty gold." They had gathered some convincing evidence that the company was getting their gold from mines that were not adhering to minimum mining standards. The reason they made an appointment to see me was they wanted to ask what could be done about this terrible situation. They were considering picketing the presentation or mounting a campaign to discourage their classmates from buying class rings from this company.

This was one time where I was very fortunate to have a reputation with the students about believing that they should have a voice. These three girls had come to see me about a matter they cared deeply about, but more importantly, they were coming to enlist my suggestions and help. They trusted that I would see their issue as an important one and would not dismiss their concerns. Without that trust and their willingness to have a conversation with me, this story could have had a very different ending than the one you are about to read.

During our meeting, I was able to empathize with their concerns, validate the need to take immediate action, and ask them to consider giving the ring company a chance to respond to their concerns before they planned a protest. In part because of their belief that I was on their side, they agreed to let me contact the company representative and schedule a meeting prior to the ring presentation.

When I called the ring representative asking that he come in and meet with some concerned students and me about his company's mining practices, I received an immediate response. It was clear that this person was going to take my students' questions and concerns very seriously. He adjusted his schedule and was in my office the next day ready to meet with the three girls. Although he had researched the question and brought a lot of information with him, he first started by asking the girls to explain their concerns. It was great that he was willing to listen to them before sharing his information. The students, in turn, were very kind and respectful. Although somewhat shy and embarrassed by the situation, they emphatically expressed displeasure with what they had discovered about the way this company acquired its gold. I was anticipating a rebuttal by the company representative, but instead he validated their concerns and assured them that he had gone to the very top of his company's chain of command to find out more about this.

What he discovered was that his company was listed among the handful of powerful companies in the jewelry business that had not yet agreed to curtail acquiring their gold from suppliers who employed "dirty" mining practices. He told us that his company was in the process of clarifying acceptable mining standards before agreeing to join the program. He explained that his company was going through research and planning with the ultimate goal of jumping onto the "clean" mining wagon, but this was an extremely complex situation. He carried with him a letter from one of the company's higher-ups assuring the girls that the company would not be using any gems coming from "dirty" mines. The girls seemed willing to take a wait-and-see attitude in regards to the ring sales at school, believing that the company would eventually get it right.

Several weeks later, we received a letter from the company announcing that the work had been completed and that they were no longer on the list of companies using "dirty gold." The letter also thanked the three girls for raising this issue as they believed the situation was resolved quicker because of their directly and respectfully well-voiced concerns. In the end, our three students felt that they had made a contribution to the gold-mining industry. I felt that the student's willingness to pursue this was somehow related to our student voice initiatives, and that the company appreciated the fact that this was handled so well by our school. Instead of exercising their rights by protesting and creating quite a scene, our students maturely and respectfully worked through the issue. It was not only a golden example of democracy at work, it was also an example of how these students did not abuse the freedoms they were given.

"It Is About Them" Revisited

Earlier, I mentioned attending RSVP training in Washington, D.C., in April of 2007 with one of my students. During our trip, Julie, a sophomore, gave me further insight into the importance of the many points raised in the first part of this chapter. Julie was a very successful student at our school, among the top-ranked students in her class. I barely knew her before our lengthy drive to the airport and the flight to D.C., which included a brief layover in Philadelphia. In fact, all I really knew about Julie was that as an eighth-grader she and her parents had given strong consideration to attending a private school instead of Kennebunk High School.

A small percentage of the eighth-grade students in our district do attend private school each year after they weigh the benefits of attending private school compared to a comprehensive public institution. As we were getting acquainted, the first thing I learned about Julie was that she absolutely loved our school and was convinced that her choice to attend her community high school was a great one. She spoke of how four of her best friends from middle school had decided to go away to school and that, in her opinion, only one seemed to be doing okay.

Her other friends seemed unhappy about their choice. She, on the other hand, was thrilled with all her teachers, the curriculum she had been exposed to, and the plan she had been developing to complete her high school experience. Whenever I asked her a question about our school and the challenges that we face, she came back with a totally positive outlook. "Oh my God, I love the student voice programs at our school," she said in response to a question I asked her about negative student behavior. When I asked about her future plans, she jumped at the opportunity to praise her teachers and the course of studies she was following to prepare her for a future in the field of medicine or education.

When we arrived in D.C and she interacted with other tenth-graders from around the country, she displayed a depth of understanding about student engagement and citizenship that showed she attended a school where students are intimately involved with many aspects of their academic experience. Julie could be a poster child for the many ideas brought forth in this book up to this point. She clearly is a participatory member in the educational process and has an inner magic that is highlighted in the last stanza of Keith Harvie's poem, "Wizard."

When she talked about her learning experiences in rigorous courses she had taken during the first two years in high school, she embodied the ideas presented in sections three and four, of learning by doing, and starting small and up-scaling as she progressed through high school.

As I got to know her better, it became clear that this was a young lady who wanted to make a difference in her school and community. A young lady who cares about others, her learning, and her school. Even before she attended the RSVP training, she was already a strong advocate for student voice and student-centered learning.

I found it deeply gratifying that a student in our school, a student that I barely knew before our trip together, could so clearly symbolize the outcomes that I believe schools should strive for in each student. In all probability, Julie is a student who would be successful in any school, yet she attends a school that pays significant attention to the idea of creating a school for each student. She is attending a school that is trying to help her find ways to become relevant. We are in a mutually beneficial situation. Our school is about her and she is responding magnificently.

It is especially gratifying when I hear validation for what we are doing from graduates. I recently received a letter from a graduate that reinforces the importance of our "school for each student" approach. Ben felt compelled to write me a letter following an experience he had in one of his college seminars. He reported that his class had read an essay about their generation that led to a discussion about their educational experiences at their respective high schools. A portion of Ben's letter follows:

> ". . . Our ensuing conversation in class revealed some astounding details about high school life across the country. My classmates detailed how their high schools were run. They were basically on lock down, set to a strict schedule, and had no flexibility with their education whatsoever. My peers' high schools were dictatorships, where whatever the principal said, was law. One student even said that her high school had painted the walls a certain mauve color, the same

color they used in prisons, because studies showed that it was conducive to learning and good behavior. When I outlined my high school career, that of independent learning, flexible scheduling, and a "school for each kid", my classmates and professor were stunned. They could not believe how much freedom I had in planning and executing my high school education. The fact that I had taken independent studies, done an internship, and had experience with online classes was something that my classmates had never heard of before.

After hearing tales of other high schools around the country, I consider myself very lucky to have attended Kennebunk High School. I knew that we had a great school, but I never how great I had it until I talked to others about their experiences. I want to thank, applaud, and congratulate you and the faculty and staff for truly making Kennebunk High School a "school for each kid." The collaboration between the administration, faculty, and students allowed my peers and I to receive the best education possible. My classes and experiences at KHS have absolutely prepared me for college life and classes; especially knowing what others around me have gone through.

I certainly hope that Kennebunk High School continues to provide such a high quality, enriching education to all who pass through its halls. We are truly lucky to have such a great school in our community". . . .

Ben's words seem to provide a great way to wrap up the opening two chapters of this book. Schools should be about them and we should provide them opportunities for voice!

Chapter 2: Discussion Questions

1. When did you first discover your voice? Who encouraged you to develop it and has that affected how you work with young people?
2. Spend four or five minutes reflecting and writing about a peak learning experience you have benefited from. Explore which of the key points advanced in the first two chapters were imbedded in that experience?

3. What are some ways that schools can advance student understanding of the relationship between individual rights and community responsibilities?
4. How can a "school for each student" approach be more successful than "a school for all students" approach at increasing academic achievement? Why?
5. Why would it be important for administration to work closely with teachers in the effort to provide more opportunity for student leadership in the school? What might some of those opportunities be?
6. Can schools become laboratories of democracy? How would you start promoting the civic mission of schools one student, one classroom at a time? What resources would you need?
7. What current practices in the school would need to change or be discontinued in order to implement the "school for each student" model? What barriers would exist if these actions were pursued?

Chapter 3

What Matters Most

"Believe that you have it and you have it."
—Latin Proverb

It seems to me that everyone's life story has been heavily influenced by a relationship of some sort. Whether a parent, coach, mentor, or teacher, everyone I know can name a person who has had a dramatic impact on their life. Their influence can be constructive or harmful, but this book is about hope and possibilities, so let's focus on the positive ones.

I immediately come up with at least six key people who have greatly influenced my life: my parents, a high school basketball coach, a high school English teacher, a college professor, and an inspirational principal that I encountered early on in my teaching career. If we consider that our parents are our first teachers, it is quite revealing that all of these people are educators.

This chapter will consider the interpersonal side of education and the relationships that educators forge with their pupils. Arguably, not much else is possible in terms of student outcomes if the adults in our schools cannot impact youth in deeply personal ways. We must "hook" students in order for them to make progress, and that hook is usually an emotional bond.

Throughout my career, I have strongly advocated for educators to put the needs and interests of each student at the forefront of their work. This foundational principle is built upon first having a strong relationship with the student. The development of this relationship is what matters most.

A Persuasive Profession

While presenting a workshop on inspirational leadership at a conference in Providence, Rhode Island, I was reminded of the far-reaching impact of educators. A woman on staff with the Brown Alliance, an educational agency connected with Brown University, told me a story that underscores the importance of educators in students' lives. She started the conversation by saying that while she knew nothing about me, she was very familiar with the work of my wife, Sharon. She stated that her twenty-one-year-old daughter had directed her to mention the fact that Sharon had been her third-grade physical education teacher more than a dozen years earlier. At the time, Sharon required her students to create an aerobic exercise routine to music as part of their P.E. class. The woman went on to say that her daughter is now living in California and working as a very successful aerobic instructor, and wished to send her former teacher a thank-you for inspiring her to take up aerobics instruction as a career. She said almost nothing about me, but provided me with a great lead-in to my presentation. I had little trouble stressing to conference participants that teachers really do touch lives by providing support, encouragement, growthful challenges, and inspiration. While teachers are often credited with affecting educational and career goals, they also greatly influence the values, ethics, character, and interpersonal skills of their students.

Last spring, some staff members at Kennebunk High School received a letter that helps illustrate the variety of ways students are influenced by their teachers. The letter, from a young man in his late thirties, praised his former teachers for helping him not only with the academic aspects of school, but also for shaping him into a hard-working, motivated employee later in life.

He started out by mentioning an English teacher who had given him a "D" on a writing piece and how that grade had forced him to confront his mediocre skills. He indicated that he now uses written language constantly in his work and how his teacher can take some credit for his success. He also wrote of how this same teacher suggested that instead of reading his 53rd Louis L'Amour western of the year he might consider reading

The Count of Monte Cristo. He alluded to how this encouragement truly changed his life. The young man continued by praising his science teacher. He remembered how this particular teacher made science fun while REALLY teaching it. While admitting that wave simulators and Vander graph generators have not featured in his life like reading and writing have, he indicated that thinking about things scientifically and mathematically certainly has. He stated how his high school science experiences forces him to slow down a bit; search for evidence and find a more thoughtful path. Finally, he thanked his former Spanish teacher for cutting him a break at the end of his senior year, while he suffered from "a nuclear case of senioritis". This alum seemed to have received vastly different gifts from each of the three teachers. He stated that sometimes being tough was what was needed, while sometimes it was being soft. One teacher had held him accountable and introduced him to new possibilities, another teacher cut him some necessary slack, and a third made him look at the world with a scientific eye.

Reading about the success of their former student provided these teachers with a refreshing reminder of the positive impact they can have on a student's life. Yet, the fact that these positive effects can happen as deeply and as lastingly as his letter depicts begs the question, "Why can't this be expanded to impact every student?" Are all students not facing similar issues? Students should be pushed to achieve greater success, determined by their personal best, and every student would benefit from mentoring as they face the hard questions, choices, and challenges of adolescence.

This inspirational letter reminds me of a successful venture I undertook as a twenty-four-year old, and how the influences of many of my former teachers made it possible. I had secured a teaching and coaching job in another part of the state and needed to find suitable housing for my young family. However, my teaching salary was so low (amazing how little has changed in 30+ years!) that we could not afford to buy or rent a house that was even remotely appropriate. We decided that the only way we could have a home that was acceptable was to build our own, so we built our house using "sweat equity" as a down payment. It is important for readers to know that I possessed little skill and aptitude for home construction. Fortunately, in the course of my twenty-four years, I had been given the gift of a "can–do" attitude and the ability to forge ahead despite the fear of failure. Although much of the credit for my confidence and courage to take such risks goes to my folks, teachers and coaches deserve some of the thanks as well. Coaches taught me that through hard work and hustle I could make a contribution on a basketball team, while teachers taught me that I could accomplish more than I originally believed I could in numerous disciplines. These traits carried over into my personal life and have driven me to ever-higher levels of success.

As I reflect back on that pivotal experience, it is easy to see that the decision to build a home was a risky venture undertaken at a tough time in my life. I not only survived, I thrived by asking questions, working through trial and error, and staying focused on possibilities. Our formidable experiences shape who we become, and teachers can play a huge role in not only simulating those experiences, but also helping us navigate and ultimately triumph over them.

Educators need to understand that the value they have in shaping who their students become is more important than the subjects they teach. Helping our students to trust in their own unique abilities and the promise of their dreams can be our greatest contribution.

Unfortunately, this reality is often buried in the rubble of state and federal mandates, test scores, and other external challenges. By overemphasizing these areas, we run the grave risk of having smart kids who cannot think freely and students of limited skills unable to aspire to greater outcomes. If education is ever going to break the grip of these external forces, it has to start by honoring what matters most: the development of a caring relationship with each student. This relationship can then make everything else possible. We must recognize the awesome gifts and responsibilities that our persuasive profession provides us.

Keep Each Candle Burning

As much as we have to accent and elevate the persuasive aspect of teaching, we must also guard against its antithesis: teachers becoming a destructive force for students. From the demoralizing put-downs and disrespectful tones that a small percentage of teachers use with students to casting a more subtle doubt over a pupil's promise and ability, we can unintentionally create a black hole for our children.

I have attended conferences where Russ Quaglia[1] spoke of our responsibility as educators to be heroes for our students and that we have a non-negotiable obligation to believe in them so they, in turn, can have higher aspirations. I have often heard Todd Whitaker[2] speak at conferences of how important it is that teachers never raise their voice, argue with a child, or be disrespectful towards them. Both Russ and Todd believe, and I agree, that doing these things nine times out of ten is unacceptable. We need to be heroes and act appropriately around students ten times out of ten.

As powerful as the positive influence of a great teacher can be for a student, we cannot lose sight of the reality that they can also cut a student down at the knees with just one negative comment. My career in education exposed me to countless instances where adults were guilty of tearing students down instead of building them up. Someone once said that it takes one hundred good comments to erase just one hurtful one. Telling students that they are not college material or that they do not have the skills necessary to take on a more challenging course are, unfortunately, regular occurrences in our schools. I have seen teachers inadvertently contribute to a child's feeling of inadequacy even as they ineffectively attempt to motivate the student. I have seen students enter high school convinced that they have no skills and no worth. Schools that relentlessly address the importance of how teachers talk to and about their students have the right idea. It comes back to a spirit of possibility and hope. Each and every student deserves nothing less.

---

[1]Quaglia, Russell. Quaglia Institute for Student Aspirations, www.qisa.org/about.php
[2]Whitaker, Todd, www.toddwhitaker.com

We must recognize the impact that our actions can have on a child's development. The following Haim Ginot poem aptly captures this concept.

*I've come to a frightening conclusion
that I am the decisive element in the classroom.
It's my personal approach that creates the climate.
It's my daily mood that makes the weather.*

*As a teacher, I possess a tremendous power
to make a child's life miserable or joyous.
I can be a tool of torture
or an instrument of inspiration.
I can humiliate or humor, hurt or heal.*

*In all situations, it is my response that decides
whether a crisis will be escalated or de-escalated
and a child humanized or de-humanized.*

—Haim Ginot

There is a flip side to the practice of ensuring that each student's candle burns brightly. We also have a responsibility to honestly appraise student achievement and not sugarcoat facts in order to inflate a student's self-esteem. The secret is to be truthful without being harsh. We must strike a balance between recognition and praise, and constructive criticism by being aware that learning and personal growth are a process and a journey.

As a high school principal, my worst days often occur as a result of the phenomenon in education that seems to force us into classifying students based on academic achievement. Who gets into the National Honor Society and who does not has often makes me question the wisdom of having such a program. How does the celebratory recognition of 20 inductees compare to the devastation experienced by the 10 students who do not get selected? Similar feelings crop up for me when we look at class rank or gifted and talented identification. We invest so much in an imperfect grading and evaluation system that we must find ways to protect students from the harm that these well-intended programs can cause. I heard Doug Reeves[3] at a conference making the point that assessment should be more like a physical than an autopsy, and we should heed his advice. We should use praise and recognition judiciously while keeping a careful watch for the potential damage we could unknowingly cause. Applying the principle from the Hippocratic Oath—first do no harm—makes perfect sense in our interactions with developing students.

[3]Douglas B. Reeves, www.makingstandardswork.com

You Are Just Getting Started

Helen Keller once said that "no pessimist ever discovered the secrets of the stars or sailed to an uncharted land or opened a new heaven to the human spirit." As I reflect on that quote, I am reminded of a huge sign over a primary school physical education teacher's door that read, "I CAN'T DO THAT YET . . . BUT I'LL TRY." What a great motto for young students to embrace. A grand lesson exists in those eight words. School is supposed to be challenging; if it were easy, there would be no lasting benefit. I love the idea that great teachers make hard work appear easy while stretching the development of our young people to the limit and beyond.

There is a story I am reminded of about a father who maintained an extraordinarily positive outlook on most everything his two young children encountered. If his ten-year-old son struck out in a little league game, you could hear him shouting, "Don't worry, Son, you are just getting started!" Several days later at another game, his son smacked a home run and as he rounded the bases to cheers and applause, you could hear his dad shouting, "Way to go, Son, you are just getting started!" The same enthusiastic chant was heard if one of his children brought home a poor grade on a vocabulary quiz. "That is okay, Son, you are just getting started." After his children were grown, this wonderful father sadly became ill and lost a battle with cancer, leaving his wife by herself. Their mother took the loss very hard and went into a lengthy, deep depression. Nothing, including the love of her children, the encouragement of her friends, or the advice of counselors and spiritual supporters could help break her free from this dark place.

Just as things looked irreversibly dark, she had a dream in which her husband said, with great love and tenderness, "You will be okay, honey. Remember, you are just getting started." Her dream provided her with enough reassurance and optimism to break out of her depression and start rebuilding her life.

Our students constantly need to be told that they are just getting started and that if they cannot do something yet, with hard work, they will eventually get it. We need to believe in them and become beacons of hope for their ultimate success. My experiences, both in how I responded when teachers believed in me, and how my students respond to my belief in them, are proof of the success of the formula: Through hard work and the support of educators, success is inevitable. At one of my high schools that had a strong tradition of adhering to strict prerequisites for entrance into Honors and AP coursework, a simple but conscientious word change serves to illustrate this formula and its success.

Many eyebrows rose when we announced that we were taking the word "required" out of our description of class prerequisites for honors-level and advanced-placement courses and replacing it with the word "recommended." Many members of our faculty were fearful that under-qualified students would flood their courses and standards would need to be lowered. Other teachers and I insisted that students should be given equal opportunities to try challenging courses and teachers should assume the responsibility of maintaining high standards, regardless of who took the course. Data carefully collected over the next several years greatly dispelled the fears of our doubtful staff. The research showed that even though "average" students took rigorous course offerings, scores on AP exams rose dramatically.

The startling results convinced most of the doubters that students can rise to higher expectations. The statistics in Figure 6 show a three-fold increase in the number of students taking AP classes from a five-year average of 38 students in 2004 to 110 students in 2007.

Figure 6: Advanced placement participation data

	Number of Students Taking AP Classes	Number of Tests Taken
1999–2004 (5-year average)	38	54
2005	73	112
2006	92	140
2007	110	161

Three times more students are taking AP Classes
and three times more exams are being taken

Not only did our enrollment in AP courses soar, the test results of our students continued to improve. The following chart illustrates how our scores compared to both the national averages and the state of Maine's averages. Keeping in mind that, on AP exams, 5 is the highest score possible, 30% of test-takers at K.H.S. scored 5s, compared to the national average of only 14%. The trend continued among students earning a score of 4; 38% of our AP students earned a 4, compared to the national and state averages of 20%. Over the past two years, an extraordinary 68% of the students we tested scored 4s or 5s on their AP exams. (See Figure 7.)

The practice of imposing artificial limitations on our students' potential began to diminish as our students experienced greater success in the AP program. We still have a ways to go in my school to truly live up to our mission statement but, as they say, "We are just getting started!"

Figure 7: 2006 and 2007 AP test score comparisons breakdown of scoring for all students tested.

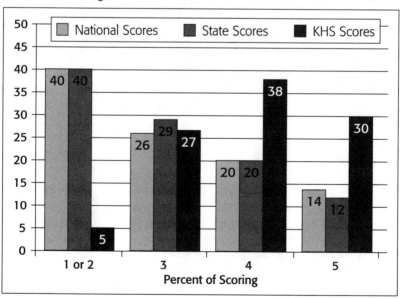

Mission Statement

*Kennebunk High School is committed to providing
a varied and rigorous academic program.
Within a safe and caring environment, each student
will be encouraged to realize his/her fullest potential
and become a life-long learner, as well as
a responsible member of society.*

In order fulfill our mission statement, particularly in reference to *each* student, our school should have one hundred more students taking AP courses and AP exams.

Even if a large majority scored 1s and 2s, we would still perform above national averages. Given the amount of energy, time, and attention spent on removing the barriers that prevent all students from experiencing rigorous learning experiences, at least we are moving in the right direction.

I was fortunate during my childhood to have people who believed in me and felt that I would eventually accomplish great things. As I struggled to swim against the current of self-doubt, fearing that I could not do certain things, others' belief in me helped to overpower my personal worries. In this sense, educators have an obligation to be cheerleaders for their students. They need to find ways to build students' confidence in their abilities and to guide them through times of struggle and confusion. Students will respond when they know people care and have faith in their abilities. They will work to prove or fulfill what people believe they can do. It makes perfect sense to expect the best for each student, but it also makes perfect sense to remind them that they are just getting started.

Three Gifts in One

In the summer of 2005, a recently retired principal from Utah told me about an idea that she had heard a neighboring principal use to boost staff morale. I was so impressed with the idea that I immediately decided to borrow it and use it with my staff. The positive outcome of this simple, but powerful, idea warrants mention here.

On the first day of school, I asked my staff to write the name and address of a living person who had had a special influence on their personal development on an index card and give it to my assistant. Someone who had had an influence on who they have become, knowing that many would mention a parent, teacher, or coach. I then asked my secretary to follow-up in the coming weeks to ensure that everyone gave us the information. No one asked why I wanted this information, but if they had I would have answered cryptically, "It is a harmless surprise." No one other than my secretary knew about my plan. In early December, several weeks before the holiday break, I wrote a letter to each person that my staff had mentioned on their cards. The following represents the content of the eighty letters we wrote and mailed.

Dear _____

This letter of appreciation is being sent to you because _____ *mentioned you as a person who has had a positive influence on his life.* _____ *works at Kennebunk High School and makes a similar contribution to a number of students here daily. As a way of thanking* _____ *for making a difference, I thank you for the role you have played in his/her development. May your holidays be filled with love, laughter, and fulfillment.*

Sincerely,

Nelson H. Beaudoin

The results of this simple gesture were astounding. I received dozens of responses from the recipients expressing how touched they were by the letter. For some, particularly the retired teachers, coaches, and staff members' parents that were named, I could not have dreamed up a better holiday gift. My staff had long forgotten the index cards they had filled out in August, so they were incredibly surprised and delighted when they started receiving telephone calls, e-mails, and cards of praise and thanks from their mentors for having mentioned them in such a positive way.

This simple idea, which took so little effort, had a huge effect on my staff. More than a year after the letters were mailed, I continued to receive comments from staff and letter recipients. Following are some samples of the cards and notes we received.

Mr. Beaudoin:

Your letter of Dec. 5 was a total and pleasant surprise. Your school and staff have been blessed to have had _____ on the front lines. I genuinely had fun teaching my students and have been satisfied with the results.

I find it hard to help out now because schools seem over-burdened with externally applied requirements that get in the way of creative and targeted teaching.

Best to you both in 2007.

Retired teacher

* * * * * *

Dear Nelson Beaudoin,

I was so happy to receive your letter about my daughter _____.

I have often wondered if anyone realized and appreciated all the time and effort she puts into her work. She is very conscientious and knowledgeable in her work and I am so proud to have her as one of my daughters. I think Kennebunk High is fortunate to have her on staff and I thank you so much for your letter.

I wish you a wonderful Christmas and a blessed new year.

Sincerely,

Parent of a teacher

Dear Nelson,

Thank you for your letter of appreciation. Every good parent strives to have a positive influence on their child, but then seeing them being acknowledged and appreciated is the real reward. _____ is certainly a treasure in my heart. My very best holiday wishes to you and your family.

Sincerely,

Parent of a teacher

* * * * * *

Nelson,

I wanted to let you know that the letter received by my aunt over Christmas was outstanding. It made her holiday and was greatly appreciated.

Thank you,

Staff Member

* * * * * *

Dear Sir,

Thank you for your recent letter with respect to _____ and my influence on his life. I am very pleased that you are keenly aware and appreciative of _____ positive influence on the lives of his students. As _____ winds down a distinguished career in teaching, he will be sorely missed and long remembered by all those who were fortunate enough to have been touched by him. For over 40 years, he has been a treasure in my life.

Sincerely,

Friend of a teacher

* * * * * *

Nelson,

I have been meaning to thank you for the letter you sent my mother. It was very thoughtful and meaningful to her. I think it was a great way to show appreciation for all the things she has done. I have told her many times, but coming from an outside person was even more powerful.

Thank You,

Teacher

* * * * * *

Hi Nel

I had breakfast with _____ on Wednesday, and she told me about the letters you sent to the people the staff had identified as having had an impact on their lives. I thought that was such a wonderful idea, and would love to steal it for my staff next year. Is that OK with you?

District Administrator

In addition to cards and letters, I had many positive conversations with staff members once the letters of appreciation flooded in. These conversations gave me many opportunities to remind my staff of the importance of the relationship side of their work and to highlight it by really personalizing it for each of them. One teacher told me that his mentor was ill and living out his remaining days in a nursing home. When this 93-year-old retired teacher and coach received his letter, he broke into tears of joy.

That heartwarming story alone made the entire project worthwhile. There are three gifts that arise when something like this occurs; it honors the person receiving the card, it values the work of the person on your staff whom the card acknowledges and, it honors the teaching profession. This was a great way to get this all-important relationship side of teaching center stage. As educators, our real value is not the content we deliver, the programs we organize, or the lessons we impart. Our lasting value lies in the relationships we forge. Mentoring young people, making a difference in their development, or being a role model is where teachers can find their true value and education can bank on continued success.

Relationship-building is at the heart of what is great about those whose life's work is teaching young people. Nothing can replace the impact that teachers have on their pupils' development, even though this does not always show up on test scores. Instead, it comes out over time in the form of students leading successful lives. Quality teaching depends on personal interactions—how teachers truly impact their students. If we truly believe that success will happen for our students, it will!

The Wallop of Time

Years ago, I happened upon Oprah interviewing Barbara Walters and her daughter on Oprah's talk show. The conversation centered on the celebrity life that Walters lived and how it affected her relationship with her daughter. At one point, either Barbara or her daughter mentioned that they had been together for all the important things, such as recitals, graduations, and birthdays, implying that creative scheduling had occurred in order to offset Barbara's extremely busy professional schedule. Then one of them threw in a qualifier by noting that while they were together for all the important dates, that was not what builds relationships. What cultivates rich relationships are the unimportant times they spent together, the quiet times, such as sitting on the beach or sharing a long drive together. They went on to acknowledge that they missed some of those times.

That small qualifier, which was part of a much longer interview, really stuck with me. As we explore the importance of relationships in helping us achieve educational success, remember the idea that some of the quiet, uncelebrated times are vital to achieving our goals. I feel there is a strong correlation between the amount of time spent together and the quality of the relationship that is forged.

The effort to create a strong adult connection for each student has led to the inclusion of advisory programs in many schools across the country. In my experiences, advisory programs have been huge assets in developing strong connections between students and a caring adult. Yet, the success of the advisory programs I implemented in five different schools were not nearly as dependent on an elaborate curriculum or special staff training as they were on a simple variable: time.

I found that putting a small group of students with an adult on a daily basis for an extended amount of time (18–20 minutes) strengthens relationships. Faculties and administrations around the country search for ways to make their advisory program stronger, yet often miss the secret ingredient that the Walters interview revealed: the magic of time. The unstructured time, the quiet time, the time with dead air can serve to develop strong ties between adults and students. The concept of time being a critical factor for student/adult bonding was highlighted in a big way during a recent experience I had facilitating a sophomore boys' group.

As the 2005 school year was winding down, a teacher representative of our Student Assistance Team (SAT) approached me about starting a sophomore boys' club at Kennebunk High School. The SAT is a group of teachers who work with referred students who are experiencing difficulty at school. The team investigates why these students are struggling academically or socially and works to develop action plans to support them. In many ways, the program acts as a pre-referral to the Special Education program.

The idea of a sophomore boys' group or club grew out of concern that the SAT team had for a couple dozen ninth-grade students who did not appear to be adjusting well to our school. They had poor-to-average grades, did not seem to like school, and most staff felt that these particular students were headed for a rough sophomore year. The idea of forming a group that would meet periodically with the school's principal was inspired by another organization in our school that had received a lot of notoriety- a group called the Captain's Club.

The Captain's Club, actually a class, was run by our superintendent of schools, Dr. Thomas Farrell. In it, twenty-four of our top students met weekly with Dr. Farrell to learn leadership and decision-making skills. In order to become a member of the group, the students were required to sign a contract to remain drug-free. Farrell, who has a long and impressive resume of working with drug education programs, had created an extremely popular club at our school. After several years, this program became so popular that a second group was started for younger students. The success of this innovative model led our SAT to explore the idea that other students, specifically a group of sophomore boys, might benefit from a similar program.

The teacher who initially asked about the possibility of starting such a group drove home the fact that these students were not connected to our school in a way that our "school for each student" mission hoped for. He made a compelling case, and I agreed to take on the challenge of creating a special group for these sophomore boys. Truth be known, I had no idea what I would do with these students, but the goal of improving their connection to our school was compelling. I started by inviting each of the 24 referred students to meet with me individually over the summer. I asked them to join our group based on the simple promises summarized by the following list. Their successful participation would lead to a ¼ credit. They would need to:

1. Attend class during late start Wednesday; students do not start classes until 9:00 AM on Wednesdays to provide professional development time for our teachers.
2. Let me, only slightly, into their academic world.
3. Complete a service project as a group in order to help them get a head start on the 30-hour community service graduation requirement.
4. Allow me to help them academically and personally by exposing them to resources I had available to me as principal.
5. Participate in a fun culminating activity.

Of the two dozen boys interviewed, fourteen joined the group and thirteen stayed active throughout their sophomore year. The program was a solid success based on the fact that ten of the boys dramatically improved their academic standing, while two stayed the same and only one did not perform as well or better than the previous year.

The reasons for the success of this program, however, had little to do with my work. In fact, on most Wednesdays as I prepared to leave the house for work, I dealt with the frustration that I (again) had nothing planned for my group. Of the thirty or so classes we had, only about half had meaningful activities planned. For example, I had the students do four or five classes of activities around career exploration that culminated with them having one-on-one meetings with community mentors who worked at their preferred career. Perhaps another five classes focused on academic goals, such as discussing progress reports, looking at test-taking strategies, and helping them better understand and apply specific study skills. We also took several field trips, one to a local factory to talk about job possibilities and another to a ropes course to do some group trust-building activities. The remainder of the groups' activities for the year were fairly unstructured, oftentimes just talking informally or playing board games.

As we tried to figure out why this group experienced success despite my obvious lack of consistent planning and organization, we kept coming back to one conclusion: I had given these students the gift of time. They were more successful for one simple reason: someone had spent quality time with them. The students did not seem to mind that the activities were not highly prearranged or particularly engaging; they responded simply because someone was willing to spend time with them. Many of the parents of these students reported how much the student looked forward to our meeting times. Some of the greatest connections with these students took place during downtime rather than during the highly organized activities.

As we work to build relationships in our schools, we need to remember the point I learned as I listened to the interview Oprah did with the Walters. Relationships grow best, not when they are fully orchestrated, but instead when there is enough time for people to interact meaningfully. We often are better-served by the unstructured activities as we strive to create relationships with our students.

The Other Side of Education

While this section could have easily fit in several other chapters, I chose to place it here because educators need to know and understand that a significant piece of what schools do for students has little to do with content knowledge. There is a whole other side of education that shares the limelight with great literature, mathematical formulas, and philosophy. There is a side of education that motivates students to come to school, that captures their hearts and minds and instills important lessons that transfer into the academic arena. This other side of education includes just about everything in school that happens outside of the classroom and many out of the ordinary things that happen in the classroom. To list all the possibilities that qualify for the other side of education would be a lengthy ordeal, so let me provide a small sampling.

In one elementary school, the entire faculty participates in an Around the World program and adopts and honors a country by integrating it into their curriculum. Many middle schools and high schools offer athletic programs, academic clubs, and co-curricular programs in drama, music, and other art programs.

Schools also stage special events, such as assemblies, dances, carnivals, science fairs, and homecoming parades. Within the classrooms at all grade levels, efforts by teachers create opportunities for guest speakers, field trips, historical reenactments, or theme-based projects. Recognizing that this is just a sample of the enormous list of possibilities that exist in schools to involve students in unique ways, let us examine why this is such an important area for teachers to pay attention to.

Perhaps the greatest reason for paying attention to these special events and opportunities for students is the recognition that they have a magical ability to secure bonds of commitment, interest, and involvement in school and in their lives outside school walls. Students care deeply about their athletic programs or their involvement in a musical and for many students, it becomes their identity at school. Bringing us back to the song mentioned in Chapter 1, page 4, it is the beat that they march to. These students form strong bonds with advisors, coaches, mentors, and adults who become instrumental in helping students focus on academic goals and success as well as nurturing passion, gifts, and dreams. Special events in the classroom often create enough excitement for students that they decide to work at a higher level. A physical education teacher who organizes a Jump Rope for Heart program at a primary school promotes service and fitness for the students. Events such as these provide students with diversions, joy, and memories that can really help them succeed in school, and in life.

Teachers and administrators need to acknowledge the power of these programs and embrace their importance in accomplishing the mission of the school. If you want to connect with a young man who might seem a bit reluctant to complete his math homework, attend his lacrosse game and strike up a conversation with him about it in the next class. If you want to see a group of students committed to a project, try attending a prom committee meeting. If you are looking for a real authentic performance exhibition, attend the school musical. These are examples of the power that special events have in the educational system. I have always believed in the advice that if you cannot beat them, join them. Therefore, my work in education has led me to a deep involvement in the other side of teaching, the personal side.

I have been an organizer of events, a supporter of strong student activity programs, and a believer in providing a depth and breadth of diverse opportunities for our pupils. I recognized early on that these events meant a great deal to my students. Whenever we can get a student to commit to something with an intensity of purpose, we are providing the student with a glimpse of what behaviors and attitudes will lead to success. Any student who learns what it takes to commit to a purposeful training regime in the weight room is one step closer to understanding what it takes to succeed in the classroom.

Sadly, some of these rich learning experiences that should be made available to every student are losing ground to competing pressures. For example, tension exists between maximizing instructional time to raise test scores and allowing students to enjoy the community enthusiasm associated with a spirit week program. Budget woes jeopardize co-curricular or extra-curricular programs in the performing arts and athletics. Science teachers are trading in student excitement and the authentic learning that occurs in science fairs in hopes of increasing students' scores on standardized tests. Even programs designed to help students in areas such as bullying are being abandoned in favor of greater security. Educators must be strong advocates for these auxiliary programs.

I have always felt that winter carnivals, spirit weeks, field days, and similar fun, unifying activities are essential to schools. With care and thoughtful planning, they can co-exist with academic programming and contribute to the learning environment. Years ago, the final event of our high school's winter carnival was a very sophisticated and rigorous "college bowl" activity that pitted the brightest students in the school in an academic competition that generated even more excitement than the always-popular tug-of-war. Teachers in each discipline generated questions, acted as judges, and displayed an excitement for this program that made it a real highlight of the school year. In another school that was experiencing trouble with bullying, the faculty committed to staging a series of "challenge days" aimed at inspiring students to take responsibility for creating a kinder, more respectful school.

As teachers, we have to find ways to mix things up for our students so that their learning is not reduced to a flat-line rhythm. We want to create excitement for our students, be it through field trips, speakers, or after-school opportunities. What special contribution can you make outside of your work in the classroom? Can you be that teacher who attends all the athletic events and snaps action photos of the students and gives each senior a 12x16 picture at graduation? Can you be that teacher who volunteers to help the junior class organize the Junior-Senior Prom? Perhaps you can be that teacher who agrees to be the advisor of the Civil Rights Team at a middle school so the school can learn more about tolerance and diversity. Maybe heading up the math team or an Odyssey of the Mind team is more suited to your skills and interests. You might be the music teacher who decides that working with fifth-grade teachers and students to write and perform an original opera is a contribution you are willing to make.

The other side of education offers many rich opportunities to elevate involvement and commitment to new heights for both teachers and students. I do not know how we could ever create a school that values each student without engaging activities that take place outside the classroom. The schools of tomorrow will need these special events, programs, and activities to capture the hearts and minds of students. If we truly believe that forging relationships with students is an essential component of great schooling, we will commit our time, talents, and resources to find and fuel diverse opportunities beyond the classroom.

Chapter 3: Discussion Questions

1. Consider people who have an influence on your growth and development? What did these people do for you? Does their influence creep into your work with students?
2. What are some ways that schools can jump start the concept of promoting sound relationships between adults and students?
3. Generate a list of ways that your school promotes positive communication with students and parents? How does this compare in volume to communication that might be negative?
4. Are there ways for an administrator to monitor and reward staff members who engage students at a personal level? Would this, in turn, improve the experiences of students?
5. Discuss ways that educators can help students get the sometimes harsh-realities around accountability and responsibility without crushing their hopefulness and enthusiasm?
6. What are some examples of ways that schools can advance community understanding about the role of relationships in quality schooling?
7. What ideas can we borrow from co- and extra-curricular programs that would strengthen our relationships with students in the classroom?

Chapter 4

Teaching and Learning

"Greatest is not a function of circumstance. Greatness, it turns out, is largely a matter of conscious choice, and discipline."[1]

—Jim Collins

I cannot overstate my admiration for those who choose to teach. There are thousands upon thousands of educators throughout America who are tirelessly advancing the tenets that will be discussed here and who, through no fault of their own, fall short of their expectations because of structural barriers to teaching and learning. These teachers are suffering failing administrations, fluctuating expectations, unjust socioeconomic structures, testing pressures, a lack of adequate resources, and the absence of quality professional development. Despite these imposed liabilities, many teachers inspire, stretch, believe in and teach the students placed before them.

I can only hope that a book dedicated to creating schools for each student will confirm the commitment and passion for students that most teachers share. If each teacher out there who

---

[1]Collins, Jim. *Good to Great and The Social Sectors,* Harper Business, 2005. p. 31.

is getting it right regardless of the obstacles they face can gain some validation from this work, we can tip things for the better. I begin this chapter on expectations for teaching and learning with that hope. We may not be able to change the structures that confront us, but we can certainly strengthen our work from inside our profession.

In the final analysis, teachers trump everything. The idea that schools cannot improve unless we have great teachers in the classroom will be central to the sections that follow. We cannot hope to reach the objective of having a school for each student without supporting excellent teachers in our classrooms.

Quality education is often touted to be within the reach and responsibility of the teaching profession; a profession that is credited with playing a vital role in society, yet a profession that is underpaid, undervalued, underdeveloped, and underutilized. Much has been said and written about what is wrong with teaching: the overwhelming nature and responsibilities of the job; the unions that sometimes protect mediocrity; and the lack of support teachers receive from their communities, to name just a few challenges. I contend that if we spend more time with what is right about teaching, much of the deficits would begin to diminish and we could begin to more clearly focus on why we are here, and how best to succeed at our chosen work.

In this chapter we will explore teaching and learning from a variety of angles that will advance the mission of creating a school for each student. At the heart of this conversation lie fundamental expectations. What is it that teachers should expect of themselves and their students? I want to be very clear that expectations should not be confused with outcomes. Outcomes are graduation rates, test scores, etc.; expectations are more about the endeavor than about production. They have more to do with quality than they have to do with quantity. Having high expectations is not about working harder, or about piling more work on the students or ourselves. It is about making the work more fulfilling and meaningful and establishing patterns of success.

Several sections in this chapter have been devoted to explore how reflection and the desire to continually improve must be at the heart of our work as educators. We will look at professional development and collaboration as ways to strengthen teaching and improve learning outcomes for our students. Other sections will look at specific qualities that lead to successful teaching and skill sets that can be replicated to improve classroom practices and put students at the center of the equation.

On our best days, we can fully embrace the importance of our profession. On our worst days, our very survival as a teacher can come into question. There is certainly much more to the teaching profession than what is included in this book, but without exploring the attitudes, convictions, responsibilities, and expectations that are covered here, the journey toward creating a school for each student would be virtually impossible. Teachers are the core of education, and without a strong core, we cannot accomplish the greatness that each of our students deserves.

Ongoing Reflection

In January of 2002, I was halfway through my first year as principal of Kennebunk High School. I had been involved in a Comprehensive School Reform (CSR) grant at my previous school and hoped to help my new school qualify for a grant award, even though Kennebunk had been unsuccessful in two previous attempts at securing CSR funding. At the time, I was spending three hours each day commuting to my job and had started listening to books on tape to break the monotony of the drive. One of the books I listened to was Peter Senge's *Dance of Change*. While listening to Senge's work, I encountered an idea that would serve as a foundation for our school's grant application and as a major factor in our school's improvement plans.

The idea had to do with our school becoming a learning community. Although it seemed apparent that schools should be learning communities, we were not so sure that this was the case. Could Senge's idea of fueling organizational improvement through becoming a learning community really apply to schools? Although it was such an oxymoron, the idea of becoming a learning community was at the heart of our grant application. The grant readers must have thought that our idea had merit because we received the grant and were given an opportunity to test our presumption.

The concept of reflective learning—using active reflection to retain new material and increase learning—was central to our plan and has recently become a recurring theme in the work of many educational leaders, such as Rick and Becky Dufour, and Michael Fullen. These educational leaders, and many others, acknowledge that the development of professional learning communities should be on every school's radar screen. Fullen advances the idea of Triple P Core Components, citing personalization, precision, and professional learning as the key elements of a successful school. He states that, "You can't have personalization and precision without daily learning on the part of teachers."[2]

---

[2]Fullen, Micheal, *Breakthrough*, 2006, p. 21.

How can a school and individual teachers create targets for improvement and how can schools engage parents and the community in that process? All stakeholders need to be part of this reflective process, especially students. Thoughtful reflection can ensure that we do not shy away from discussing the tough questions. Reflection tends to expose the blind spots in the self-assessments of our work, and allow room for improvement to occur.

Getting feedback from students and parents is a time-honored and effective means of testing our assumptions about the quality of our work. Asking students whether homework assignments were reasonable in length, relevant, and contributed to their learning provides important information for the conscientious teacher. Having the courage to ask tough questions and the determination to use the information to improve our teaching practices is one example of reflective learning.

Another way to get valuable feedback about our teaching is to participate in peer reviews or observations. Having colleagues sit in our classroom and us in theirs provides a means to gather non-threatening comments and ideas about teaching practices. A set of additional friendly eyes can have a wonderfully positive impact on our work.

Ongoing reflection, however, does not require constant surveys and an inordinate number of time-consuming observation processes. All that is really required is a mind-set that each day, with each lesson, we are setting out to improve on our previous day or class. Bravo to teachers who keep a class notebook and write comments in the margins of their lesson plans after they are delivered to remind themselves of ways to improve on what they have done.

Think about the benefits that reflective learning brings to the person who practices it. Wouldn't it be energizing to know that we are not settling for being ordinary, that instead we are stretching? How lucky students would be to have a teacher who works to be better every day. What kind of growth and success model would that create for our students in terms of their behaviors?

Three Grant Goals That Worked

Kennebunk High School's CSR grant had three main goals. We first wanted to be reflective about teaching and learning. A goal that would force us to form Communities of Practice (CoP) groups. These professional discussion groups were charged with the task of looking at classroom practices to find ways to more fully engage and motivate our students. A major focal point of our grant application was the realization that our students were not very engaged in their learning. We wanted our faculty to explore whether this area of concern could be improved with teacher collaboration. How these groups were formed and evolved will be examined later in greater detail.

The second goal of our CSR application called for us to finds ways to personalize our programs so we could better meet the needs of each individual student. In fact, our motto for the grant was to create a "school for each kid." A motto that was created long before writing this book. Although "a school for each kid" appeared to be at odds with the "No Child Left Behind" legislation that was emerging, we believed that the focus on each student as opposed to all students was what was needed to improve our school. We understood that test scores were important but also knew that in the absence of a personalized approach, higher scores would be difficult to achieve or sustain.

Our third goal was closely related to the first two. We would strive to provide more student voice in our school as a way to enhance student participation, citizenship, and leadership. Over time, this straightforward focus on student voice led to many other initiatives such as becoming a First Amendment Project school, instituting student-led conferences, and revitalizing our school newspaper.

As it turned out, the three goals blended very nicely and did not create competing tensions. We were able to consistently focus on student outcomes. We summarized our intent in a brochure, "By personalizing our approach to students, by giving them a voice and by improving classroom practices, we believe we can reform our school."

These three goals also match the three criteria for creating great schools listed in this book's introduction: caring relationships, opportunities to contribute, and high expectations. Yet the scope of our work was considerably more complex than this, and the pursuit of these goals led us to much wider areas of focus. Organizational practices were adapted and adjusted to maximize our focus on each student. Our advisory program took on a different meaning, student-led conferences were started, and policies directly related to our course of studies were altered. Professional development took on a different feel as our CoP groups took hold.

Our grant called for "inside-out" reform as opposed to "outside-in" reform. Rather than bringing in consultants or replicating programs from other districts, we challenged our faculty to draw upon their own expertise to improve our school. During the three years of our grant, we made good progress in all areas. Our school implemented many changes during this time. Some of the changes, such as "dress-down Fridays" (where teachers could wear jeans as long as they donated $1 to the scholarship fund) were simple, small changes.

Others, such as opening the doors to rigorous courses to each student, or changing graduation traditions, were more challenging changes. All of the changes, big and small, were driven by the goals of our CSR grant. Whenever we faced a decision or the possibility of change, the question was run through the filter of whether or not this would advance our efforts in personalization, reflective teaching and learning, or student engagement. Baseline data we collected to measure progress over time showed dramatic improvement each year. For example, 15% of our graduates achieved honor grades prior to the grant in 2001, but five years later, the number had ballooned to 45%. (See Figure 8.)

Our objective to improve classroom practices, personalize programs, and give students voice had clearly increased the number of students who cared about their academic success. In addition to the remarkable increase in students achieving honor-roll grades, survey data from graduating seniors showed conclusively that our students were more positive about school as the baseline figure of 64% before the grant grew to 78.3% over the three-year grant period and reached an impressive 92% two years later. (See Figure 9.)

When asked whether or not school supported our students' enthusiasm for learning, a mere 26% of our students responded affirmatively to that question in 2002. Student enthusiasm for

Figure 8: Students achieving honors at graduation.

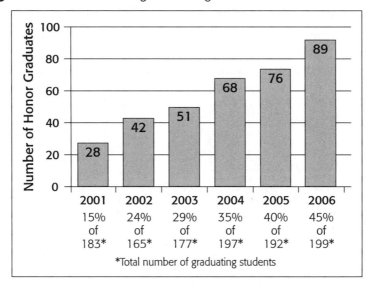

Figure 9: Graduating seniors were asked the question, "Did you have a positive experience at Kennebunk High School?"

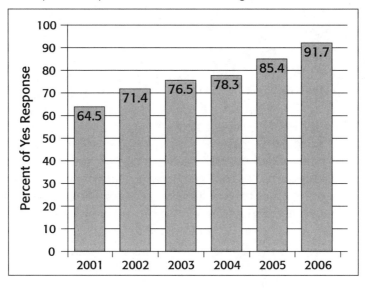

Figure 10: Graduating seniors were asked the question, "Does this school make you enthusiastic about learning?"

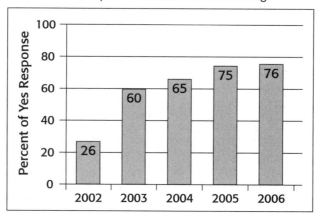

learning was an area that our grant proposal directly targeted. We hypothesized that by increasing personalization, reflecting on teaching practices, and increasing student voice that "yes" responses to the question about student enthusiasm would increase.

Surprisingly the response more than doubled during the life of the grant, and by 2006, the percentage had almost tripled. The 26% in 2002 had risen to 76% by 2006. (See Figure 10.)

The idea of becoming a learning community, which we had borrowed in part from Peter Senge, had worked in our school. We had dramatically affected not only the climate of our organization; we had also affected student outcomes. Our efforts showed up in the form of higher student achievement and additionally led to other positive changes in our organization. One of the most impressive was our approach to professional development, which will be highlighted in the following section. If schools are serious about supporting and training teachers to personalize instruction and differentiate, they must find ways to provide them with much-needed time and resources.

Communities Of Practice (CoP)

It is hard to remember what life was like at Kennebunk High School before we started professional learning groups. Not because of a memory defect, but because it is painful to recall just how fruitless our continual efforts were to create quality professional development. I suspect that my frustrated efforts, and those of my staff, to organize inspirational and meaningful in-service opportunities for the faculty mirrored what was occurring in many other schools. Once in a while, we would plan and implement a program that would meet our needs and affect our school in a positive way, but more often than not, our workshops fell short of our expectations. Rarely could we meet the needs of a significant majority of the participants and rarely were we able to sustain focus from one workshop to the next. Each program felt like a one-shot deal and the effects were short-lived. Thankfully, all of this changed with our professional discussion groups.

Today one can find many sources of support available for schools interested in creating professional discussion groups, with the Dufours' work being the most renowned. However, we wanted to create change from the inside out and consciously resisted depending on an outside model. We knew of the protocols for Critical Friends Groups (CFG) and even hired a consultant for a half day to give us a quick overview. Yet, we were determined to start our learning communities quickly and did not want to spend the time or the money for formal training. There was also a belief that if we focused too much on process, at least in the early stages, we would hinder our goal of getting teachers talking about teaching and learning. We had a grant beginning in August of 2002, and we wanted to implement groups at the beginning of the school year. Our grant served as the initial impetus for our faculty to begin this work.

Our original plan called for teams of eight teachers to spend 19 hours over the course of one year talking about teaching and learning. We set 19 hours of meeting time as a goal and promised that we would carve at least half of that time out of existing workshop time. Teachers were to take responsibility for finding the rest of the time on their own. The decision to place eight members on a team was as much a mathematical solution—64 teachers is divisible by eight)—as it was our belief that a group size of less than ten would be more manageable. We also decided that representatives from different departments would populate each team. Many of our departments had eight members and this also influenced our initial groupings; we wanted to avoid having two members from the same department on the same team. Other early decisions took into consideration team membership and facilitation. Although membership was determined randomly, there were some adjustments made to ensure that some of our strongest leaders and our most reluctant faculty members were distributed across the eight teams. These adjustments were based on hunches and although hunches are rarely 100% correct, the thoughtfulness seemed to ward off any major problems in our original groups. We enlisted eight group facilitators, providing them with a small stipend, and spent one day in early August preparing for the first several meetings.

The focus of these early CoP groups was to have teachers talk about teaching and learning and, more specifically, how to better engage our students. At our first meeting, we explained the proposed program and introduced some fundamental parameters or rules for the meetings. Chief among our expectations was that these groups were going to be a venue for positive discussions. They were not going to become negative venting sessions. Two of our first three activities focused on qualities great teachers possess. In one exercise we had each of the eight team members in groups of two read a section of *The Qualities of Effective Teachers*[3] by Sam Senger and asked them to summarize the information for their teammates. From that activity, each team was to come up with an executive summary of the book and translate the ideas from the book into the actual actions of great teachers.

Then, we carefully examined and discussed a document that had been created the previous spring involving reflections from our students about their peak learning experiences. It turns out that our students, in their attempts to describe peak learning experiences, usually focused on the qualities of their

---

[3]Strange, James H. (2002). *Qualities of Effective Teachers*, Association for Supervisors and Curriculum Development.

teachers. Interestingly, these two separate examinations of instruction—a book and our students' reflections about peak learning experiences—were remarkably similar. With this discovery, our CoP program was off to a very successful start. These two activities set a strong tone that the purpose of our CoP program was to focus on instructional practice and how to better engage our students. (A summary of the conclusions we made about quality teaching can be found on page 83.)

Our groups continued throughout the first half of the school year with positive results and, as we entered the second semester, our teachers had completed nearly two thirds of their 19 hours. Although we were being quite prescriptive about group activities and had to overcome some challenges with attendance in some groups because of coaching commitments, the CoP idea was quickly taking hold. An astounding thing happened that we had not anticipated: our faculty really began to look forward to these meetings. They were developing relationships with colleagues they normally did not interact with. The focus on freely discussing teaching and learning was a refreshing novelty for our staff. We spent time examining student work, deciphering test results, and seeking to understand concepts such as differentiation and upper-level questioning techniques.

Another outcome, which was a pleasant surprise, was that some of our teachers began to go into each others' classrooms to conduct peer observations. I had tried to encourage this practice in my two previous schools, but teachers were reluctant to participate. Now it was happening without any prompting from administration.

I first heard of this development when one of our group facilitators told me of two teachers who had agreed to go into each other's classroom. One of the teachers had a flamboyant style that students really enjoyed, but she was disorganized and a bit scattered. The other teacher was the exact opposite, wonderfully organized and detailed, but her classes often lacked spontaneity. This had such a powerful potential to help both teachers improve that I talked up the idea with the other group facilitators in hopes of encouraging more peer observations. To my amazement, other observations were already occurring, and one group had gone as far as attending one class of each of the other seven teachers in their group.

Several weeks later one of my seasoned veterans, a great social studies teacher who had always kept himself pretty isolated, came into my office to tell me that he had visited a younger math teacher's class who also had a reputation for being a good teacher. A wide smile brightened my face as he explained that the younger teacher was much better than he expected and, to his surprise, he had picked up a couple of great practices that he intended to incorporate in his own teaching. He noticed the other teacher using some motivational techniques that he wanted to try with his students. It is probably quite accurate to say that this teacher rarely sought to improve his teaching by borrowing ideas from his colleagues. He was an excellent teacher, but until our CoP experience, that excellence came to him only through private reflection and experimentation. Until then, I do not think he ever imagined that he could improve his work simply by watching another teacher.

We concluded the CoP program that first year with a required feedback survey from each teacher. In reviewing the results of the survey, we found great commonalities among our staff. They had grown to value the time together to talk about teaching and learning. Their attendance came in at 89%, averaging 17 of the targeted 19 hours of meeting time. In their feedback, most teachers reflected that they had engaged in meaningful positive dialogue about teaching and learning. Our goal of becoming a learning community was being realized. Most of the feedback indicated a need for more structured time for the meetings. Groups had been frustrated with members who had coaching commitments or college courses that conflicted, which accounted for most of the attendance challenges. Teachers also asked that we become less prescriptive about topics and activities for the groups. Although the work had been well-received and had served to create productive conversations about teaching and learning, most teachers still reported that the work had not resulted in appreciable changes in their teaching.

We entered the second year of our CoP experience committed to making the program even better. Our greatest initial excitement centered on the fact that our school committee had approved of a program designed to alleviate the frustration around structuring time to meet. The committee unanimously approved a program that we had proposed that would provide our faculty with weekly professional development time. Every

Wednesday morning, the school day for students would start at 9:05 as opposed to the customary 7:45 start time. This would provide our teachers with a weekly time to meet, a way to avoid scheduling conflicts and, most importantly, they would not be forced to sacrifice their personal time. We called this day late-start Wednesday.

Another change that we encouraged in our second year was a special focus on action items. We felt that we had talked enough about bringing changes into the classroom and now it was time to actually do it. Teachers began to engage in action research as the expectation of bringing action outcomes from the group meetings into the classroom became more clearly defined. We wanted to see tangible results in the classroom that grew directly out of our investment in CoP.

The last major adjustment we made was to allow more teacher-directed, theme-based work groups. This came about from the administration listening to teacher requests to explore and discuss areas of particular interest to them. Initially, we avoided universal activities that all the groups would want to engage in, and instead created high-interest, topic-focused groups that we called think tanks. Teachers would submit ideas for discussions and faculty members would choose a meeting that was of high interest to them. It seemed that we had discovered an even richer way to provide professional development with the freedom to explore ideas that were of special interest to individual teachers. This greatly increased their enthusiasm for the CoP program.

Our groups eventually re-formed into semi-permanent theme-based committees. For example, we had teachers interested in advancing literacy meeting as one group, teachers interested in redesigning the senior year experience as another group, while yet another group worked on improving the advisory program at our school.

I included this focus on the development and evolution of our CoP program to illustrate the importance of teacher collaboration and the idea that professional growth can occur when educators are given time and a framework to discuss their craft. This attention to professional development is a gift we made available for our teachers, but the true beneficiaries are the students.

Learning Communities

The four-plus years of experiences we have had with our CoP program has inspired our school to some wonderful outcomes. Yet, in many ways, the best improvement that has occurred in our school has been the creation of an enriching, collaborative professional climate. Staff soared after we began this program.

This improvement is deeply encouraging because one area that continues to be a challenge in educational settings, particularly at the secondary level, is the isolation of teachers. Throughout most of my career, the practice of teachers "closing the door" and working in seclusion has been the norm. Although some of this is created by individual teachers who prefer their privacy, most school structures simply do not allow for much collaboration. If teachers are not separated from one another totally, there is departmentalization that leads to segregation by discipline. This climate carries several hazards. Isolation can cause narrow perspectives and leaves teachers with little opportunity to discuss their craft. If little interdisciplinary work occurs and exemplary practices are rarely discussed, then teacher improvement is limited to individual initiative and scattered professional development activities. In extreme cases, it allows teachers to hoard great ideas and strategies so that only their students can profit. Teachers can be mediocre, or worse, and either never know it (because they have no point of reference) or never have their limitations exposed and have an opportunity to change and grow.

One of the greatest benefits created by our professional discussion groups was the impact it had on reducing teacher isolation. When teachers started sitting down together to talk about their craft, academic practices improved. As the sharing of ideas became a habit, the culture of isolation changed to one of support and collaboration. In many cases, this led to professional renewal. Our faculty, some of whom had been on automatic pilot for years, had a chance to be exposed to new ideas. Additionally, they were encouraged to try out new things in their classrooms. Although our first year did not include the amount of action research we would have liked, the concept of trying new things really started emerging in the program's second year.

We learned that action research encourages change and change happens quicker when the work occurs in a public setting. Teachers who decided to try a particular idea had the added responsibility of reporting back to their group. This added some accountability, but more importantly, it provided teachers with a support system. We also had a much stronger commitment to our school vision and mission as the activities planned for CoP meetings had a consistent focus.

That consistent focus was ultimately the students and how we could improve our work for them. Conversations about student work began to happen. Thoughtful discussions about essential learnings and common assessments became regular occurrences. Adults began to look at their work more reflectively, and the fact that this reflection occurred in a group setting made it all the more powerful.

Overseeing this work required very little effort. The leadership of the school worked to provide a climate of participatory management and to encourage the advancement of a shared vision. As we reflected on the success of our professional learning communities, just as we did the success of our students, we were provided with rich evidence that our school improvement efforts were moving us in the right direction. Kennebunk High School was becoming the learning community our CSR grant application had hoped.

Traits of Quality Teachers

On page 76, I discussed two activities our staff completed in their Communities of Practice groups that looked at, and defined, the qualities of outstanding teachers. One activity involved a common reading about effective teaching and the other was an examination of some students' reflections about their peak learning experiences. Both seemingly unrelated activities yielded essentially the same findings, which were surprisingly clear-cut. No matter how we looked at teaching during these two exercises, all of our findings fit into four essential qualities: great teachers know their students, expect a lot from them, care about their success, and are willing to support their work. It would be hard to come up with a more straightforward formula: know and care about your students, ask them to learn much, and provide the support they need to succeed. Through my many years in education, I have known hundreds of excellent teachers and every one of them possessed these essential characteristics.

With some effort we could "spin" the qualities and add complicated definitions and explanations, but why not keep it simple? The foundational characteristics of a teacher do not require a long list of qualifiers, only a few. The simple yet elegant truth is that to be respected, you must treat others with respect. If a teacher cares about his or her students, the students know it. If a teacher seeks to know a student at a more personal level, the student can sense that as well. This covers one qualifier of quality teachers, the personal side of education. Another characteristic has to do with the substance of our work: teaching and learning. The quote, "Great teachers make hard work appear easy," adequately covers the idea of expecting a lot from students but at the same time, supporting their journey to success. I have seen teachers turn that idea on its head and make learning that could be easy nearly impossible.

In my many years as a principal, I have used a variety of evaluative systems to measure the effectiveness of my staff. Three of them will be summarized here to offer some examples of how different educators determine the qualities and skills that lead to good teaching. In one district, we trained everyone based on the book, *The Skillful Teacher: Building Your Teaching Skills*, by Jon Saphier and Robert Gower.[4] The observations in this district were based on a whole series of skill sets and common vocabulary taken from the book that included attention, momentum, routines, clarity, expectations, relationship building, climate, curriculum design, and models of teaching. This is only a partial list of the book's content but it is interesting to note that all of these different perspectives on teaching fall into four broad categories: management, instruction, motivation, and curriculum.

The evaluation system we currently use in my district is one that was internally created. It is a six-page rubric that focuses on five overarching standards:

1. Teachers are committed to students and their learning.
2. Teachers know the subjects they teach and how to teach those subjects to their students.
3. Teachers are responsible for managing and monitoring student learning.
4. Teachers think systematically and creatively about their practice and learn from experience.
5. Teachers are active members of learning communities.

In the spring of 2006 the organization that publishes *The Skillful Teacher*, Research for Better Teaching Inc., conducted a workshop on teacher evaluation for the administrators in our district. They described the same four areas of performance: management, instructional strategies, motivation and curriculum planning. I particularly like the five propositions that this consulting firm advance about teaching. They claim that nothing is as important as the teacher and what continually occurs between them and their students. Secondly they believe that it is hard to imagine any job harder or more complex than teaching. From there they stress the need for research and reflection in order to provide students with the greatest opportunities to learn. Next they discuss the huge base of knowledge available to teachers while cautioning that this is not a prescriptive list of

---

[4]Saphier, Jon and Robert Gower, 1979. *The Skillful Teacher: Building Your Teaching Skills.* Research For Better Teaching, Inc., www.rbteach.com

do's and don'ts, but instead a foundation of information that can be used and adapted to fit different situations. Finally, they stress the importance of teachers talking to one another about the craft of teaching. They advance the idea that teachers can improve their craft by learning from one another. These five points underscore the belief that teaching is a perpetually growing and evolving set of proficiencies.

The fact that there are more information and evaluation systems to wade through than one could hope to read in a lifetime confirms that the craft of teaching is a very complex subject. Yet, in spite of its complexity, evaluative systems cannot hide the core truth that to be a great teacher, one has to know and care about students, hold them to high expectations for learning, and then help them succeed. We have now traveled full circle and have returned to the three necessary ingredients for successful schooling: caring, expectations, and opportunities. I marvel at how simple yet comprehensive and accurate this list of the qualities of great teachers is. Whether I look at the phenomenal band teacher at my current school or an inspirational social studies teacher I had in college, the same strengths are present. Great teachers know their students, expect a lot from them, care about them, and are willing to support them on their journey to success.

Classroom Management

It would be too limiting to have a discussion about quality teaching without also talking about the management of student behavior. Achieving success in the classroom would be unlikely without having the ability to successfully manage kids. My vantage point of working closely with nearly 500 different educators in eight school districts provides me with insights on how great teachers manage their classrooms.

For 16 of my 37 years in education, I served as the assistant principal assigned the daunting task of monitoring student behavior. What I found should not be surprising: there is a huge difference between teachers who can and teachers who cannot manage children. I also found that those teachers who are rich in their management abilities get richer, while those that are poor just keep getting poorer. I believe that those teachers who are on the lower end of the continuum relative to their skills have a harder time enjoying what they do. I wonder how some of the teachers I have known can get up each day and return to the chaos that exists in their classrooms. Teaching is a tough job that becomes even tougher when the students we are trying to reach are being difficult. Martin Haberman insists that great teachers are not very concerned with discipline; they do not have to be.

I remember sitting alone in my classroom at the end of a spring day early in my teaching career, vowing that I would hang on and simply survive the rest of the year, but that next year, I would make some BIG changes in my classroom management plans. I had tough classes that year and each day I ended feeling like I was losing the battle. Probably all teachers have been at that place sometime in their career, be it with one classroom of students or an entire assignment of classes. This is a pretty natural occurrence. Managing a classroom of young people is not a close-ended skill; it is very much an open-ended skill with countless variables, such as the ability to make tough on-the-spot decisions, and the need for endless revisions. There are some noticeable variations between teachers who achieve good classroom management and those who do not. The following offers some insights that I have gained along the way that are included to help show that subtle differences in how we approach interactions with students can lead to huge differences in how they behave.

The best place to start is with the concept of self-fulfilling prophesies. Based on countless pieces of evidence, I am a firm believer that students live up to our expectations of them, good or bad. When I address a large group of students at my school, I make a big deal out of the fact that I do not have teachers lined up along the wall, arms folded, to police their behavior. I tell the students that I want to have a school where 200 young people can listen quietly and respectfully without the need to be closely supervised. They want the same thing so they comply. I know that if there are teachers hovering over students at an assembly trying to catch them misbehaving, the students will give the teachers exactly what they are looking for. The lesson here is that teachers hold the brush that paints on the canvas called their classroom and they have options. My wife recently returned from a conference and shared that a speaker told a story that matched my beliefs about self-fulfilling prophecies. It appeared that this speaker had an overly active fifth-grader transfer into her PE class. The boy, who I will call "Killer," had pretty much destroyed her last three lessons even as she tried to force his conformity. She was faced with the option of either doing something drastic, or coming to grips with the likelihood that Killer would ruin her class for the remainder of the year.

She decided that she would publicly tell Killer how pleased she was to have him join her class and how his leadership skills and abilities added so much to what she was trying to accomplish. At first Killer was shocked and confused about this positive attention. The teacher kept at it, however, and each day she found something new to like about Killer. The story ends with Killer becoming the leader and contributing student she had expected him to be. Children, almost always, give us what they think we expect from them. One of the keys to successfully manage a classroom is to expect great behavior.

I heard another similar bit of advice at a conference years ago that has stuck with me. The speaker, who was presenting a workshop on developing a sound classroom management plan, talked about two key letters that were magical in achieving quality classroom behavior. We all laughed when he announced that those two letters were N-O, and that they spelled the word "no." He went on to explain that the word "no" was essential in dealing with a classroom of students, but was quick to point out that how you said "no" was really the magical part. If people could master the art of saying "no" *with love*, the power struggles that occur with some students would diminish significantly. For example, if a student, Suzie, asked to go to her locker and her teacher simply said, "No," my hunch is that Suzie would then ask, "Why not?" and the pathway to an escalating conflict would be paved. In the same scenario, if the teacher had responded, "No Suzie, I know this is important to you but let me finish this part of the lesson and you can ask me later," a power struggle would be much less likely to occur.

Oftentimes, much of what is categorized as student misbehavior or students giving the teacher a hard time on purpose, is misinterpreted. Rarely is the misconduct a personal thing, but that is often how it is seen. The teachers who struggle with classroom management have a knack for backing students into corners. They give students no way out, and then act bewildered when the student verbally lashes out at them. Oftentimes, what the student is upset about has nothing to do with school or the teacher, but the teacher ends up giving them a target to "go off" on. Teachers need to be ever-mindful in order to avoid putting students in situations where they lose face. Any public criticism of their behavior is likely to create a bigger problem, as will seeking an admission of guilt followed an apology in front of their peers. So if, for example, we are upset with Johnny for cutting in the lunch line and go up to him and demand that he move to the end of the line, we will probably get more than we bargained for. Johnny, who is probably suffering from low blood sugar because he needs to eat, will deny cutting or challenge us to do something about the other six kids who cut in front of him. We will probably grow more determined to not let this kid win, and up the paved road of conflict we will go, to a place that will not be good for anyone. Wouldn't it be far more meaningful to discuss cutting with Johnny after lunch in a private meeting? In that situation, we could even have him help us determine a suitable consequence. Handled in this way, Johnny is not backed into a corner, has no reason to fight us, and might just learn and internalize that cutting line is unacceptable. Even better, we will have modeled for him a mature, respectful way to resolve conflict, and how to ask others to be accountable for their behavior.

As weird as this may sound, punishment is often the problem in disciplinary situations. When faced with a challenging situation from a student, there are usually two possible responses: we can either crush the student into compliance or we can counsel the student into compliance. The word "compliance" is the common denominator in each choice and while I could cite thousands of occasions where both responses worked, I vehemently believe that forced compliance does not change behavior long-term. Johnny, the student who cut in the lunch line, also likes to run in the hall. He wants to be first at everything, first to get on the bus, and as we already know, the first one to get his lunch. The adults in the school can force Johnny into submission. He can be made to walk in the hallway because teachers can be spaced every fifty feet to monitor him, but I contend that Johnny will walk while glancing over both shoulders, looking for the time when no teacher will be watching so he can speed up. Missed recesses, detention, and calls home will not change Johnny's behavior of speeding down the hall. On one level, he just wants to get somewhere first and on another level, he is enjoying the game of running because he can agitate the teachers. He has been given power.

It is a bit slower and harder, but so much more beneficial to help Johnny come to understand that he will get home at the same time whether he runs to the bus or not, or that he will not go hungry if he is tenth in the lunch line instead of first. The focus must be to help our students understand why they need to change their behavior and to support them as they learn new behaviors and attitudes. As Johnny is counseled toward a change in behavior, it does not mean that punishments sometimes do not occur; it just means that they do not become the main focus and solution. I had a long-standing rule when it came to disciplining students: If I ever found myself getting satisfaction out of a punishment I was handing out, I knew I was doing it for the wrong reasons. Discipline can never be about revenge, or a shortcut solution in order to gain control. It has to be about educating for change and growth.

And, remember the sage advice that we really have to pick our battles. A roomful of rambunctious students presents a teacher with thousands of opportunities a day to take a stand. We have to decide if this particular hill is one to die on or if there is wisdom in ignoring certain behaviors. Those who can grow a thick skin can let a great deal go by, while those with a thinner skin seem to need to control everything. I greatly admire teachers who can accurately gauge when their actions will lead to a power struggle with a child and are able to skillfully dodge those situations. It is important not to engage in a confrontation over small issues that can just as easily and safely be ignored. A teacher who will not allow a student to enter class without a pencil is most likely giving that student an excuse for not working and for not learning. What would be the harm of having a box of extra pencils on hand and dealing with the irresponsibility and forgetfulness in a more creative and instructive way?

The last piece about classroom management has to do with appropriately ordering our priorities for student behavior. What we teach and how interesting we can make the subject certainly has some bearing on how students behave. How well we plan for transitions and how much idle time our students have also will affect their behavior. Many teachers who struggle with classroom management miss the preventative things that diminish the likelihood of problems occurring. This really leads us back to the points made earlier about the traits of quality teachers. Knowing our students well, showing them care and respect, expecting them to reach high expectations, and supporting their journey to get there will leave little time for petty power struggles. Behavioral issues are really interpersonal issues and if we, as teachers, understand that relationships are what matters most, we will create a great environment in which students can learn, free from the urge to be at war with us.

Chapter 4: Discussion Questions

1. What are some ways that schools can pay attention to ongoing reflection by professional staff? How could parents and students be involved?
2. Consider the idea of implementing peer observations among your faculty? How could this be beneficial to your students and your teachers?
3. What is your reaction to the statement that we should see students as "possibilities" rather than "problems"? How would this play out for the students in your school who are disenfranchised?

4. Considering the importance of classroom management, what processes could be put in place to help teachers support one another through collaboration?
5. Consider how student centered your classroom is on a continuum from 1 to 10, with 10 being extremely student centered? What types of supports would you need to move to a higher level? What hurdles would have to be cleared?
6. Do you and your colleagues share similar beliefs about what the mission of your school should be? Why or why not? Do the answers to these questions create obstacles school to improvement?

Chapter 5

The 12 Rs: Joining a Team

"Our ideals are our better selves."
—Amos Bronson Alcott

Following are twelve tenets as guidelines for increasing professional standards within a school. Helping teachers realize that they are in a profession that touches the world is critical, but it is equally critical that teachers understand the responsibilities that accompany such important demands.

Earlier, I mentioned the importance of educators working to change some of the negative perceptions that exist outside of the educational community regarding teachers. As unfair as you or I might think the criticism is that we sometimes receive, we must acknowledge that it exists. Acknowledging that a problem exists is the first important step toward correcting it. I offer twelve tenets of professional behavior as a reliable guide to help us create a quality school and, at the same time, to improve public perceptions about educators. I believe that the absence of any of these tenets would leave us open to criticism and diminish our ability to create quality-learning experiences for our students. As we ponder what we can do to build success in the teaching profession and as we strive to meet the needs of each student, consider carefully how these ideals could further advance our work.

1. Be **R**esolute

Success in education requires a determination that is hard to fully define. But we can begin by stating that being resolute can be defined as being determined and unwavering in the wake of the daily challenges facing us as educators. Yes, we have too many students; yes, we do not have enough resources and at times, we have unsupportive parents. These daily tests of our resolve are exactly that—tests. Educators who are resolute define the necessary stepping-stones to success and head out on the journey with a can-do attitude. Teachers know how difficult it is to stay positive and focused in the wake of all the challenges they face each and every day. Therefore, it is critically important that they believe in themselves, in their efforts, and in their students.

Finding examples of teachers who are not being resolute is a simple exercise. How often have we seen teachers bend to the pressures from students to lower academic expectations? How easy is it to find teachers who gave up on a new idea before the rationale was even explained? When have you ever witnessed a new decision implemented without a chorus of "yeah buts" and negative conversations bursting forth from disgruntled teachers? Have you ever seen a faculty or group of educators take on an issue without first trying to place blame elsewhere by stating that they will take the challenge on, but want to go on record that they did not create it?

I have heard Todd Whitaker[1] present on several occasions and I love the short bit he does on "Crab Corner," the corner that exists in every school where adults gather and complain about this or that. We need to help our teachers, particularly the young ones, understand that these circles of negativity hurt our profession. If people feel a need to vent, they should do so to people who can do something about it, and better yet, as the vent they should provide some possible solutions. Complaining

---

[1]Todd Whitaker, www.toddwhitaker.com

just for the sake of complaining passes misery from one person to another and sucks the energy out of everyone. Being resolute does not mean we never have a complaint; it just means we do not pass it on to others who cannot do anything about it except share our pain. Being resolute means we look at things through a lens of possibility rather than a lens clouded by doubt.

2. Be **R**eflective

The need to have teachers be reflective about their work is not just a frivolous idea, it is a necessity. In the business world, profit or production data can provide feedback for improvement. In education, the road signs toward improvement are less obvious. Schools can look at test scores, survey data and other accountability measures, but individual teachers need to dig a bit deeper. Teachers need to do all that they can to examine their work with the intent of making it as great as it can be. They have to constantly analyze lessons, strategies, routines and assessments, and resist the temptation to rest on previous successes. The dangerous irony here is that as soon as we think we have finally got it right, we are probably much closer to getting it wrong.

I take pride in my practice of constantly seeking better ways to accomplish things that many people would say are already successful. This attitude has put me in positions of attending many conferences and programs promoting change in education. At an early organizational meeting for Maine schools pursuing a Comprehensive School Reform Grant, I met a Science teacher who truly represents the best of the teaching profession. Erwin, as I will call him, was a 42-year teaching veteran at the high school that he had graduated from. With the exception of his four years away at college, he had been walking the halls of the same school as a teacher or student for 46 years!

At this meeting, there were a number of enthusiastic young educators exploring contemporary educational strategies to bring back to their respective schools. Erwin, because of his age, caught my attention. I could not help but think of some of the veteran staff members at my school who resist change, so I made a point of asking Erwin how all of these new ideas set with him. I asked him how a person who had been teaching science for more than four decades could get excited about these new ideas. I was certain that he could simply go to school every day on automatic pilot and no one would say that he was slacking on the job. Why was he here? Erwin said that when he made a choice to become a teacher, he made a promise to himself to never accept mediocrity. Listening to these new ideas and working to incorporate them in his work was a way for him to stay responsive and excited about his profession. Without the determination to remain vibrant, Erwin would join a large group of educators who do not incorporate reflective learning in order to improve their teaching skills. He would join a group that settles for mediocrity. We settle for mediocrity when we make education about us instead of about the students. I know that Erwin would treat the call to create a school for each student as a possibility for personal commitment and growth rather than as a personal burden. I wish more educators approached their profession the way Erwin has, a way of teaching that belongs in the doctrine of everyone who aspires to be a great educator.

3. Be Rigorous

I have consistently found that extraordinary teachers demand a lot from their students. Great teachers have high standards; they do not accept mediocrity. Yet, encircling the high expectations is a web of caring, support, and patience that builds confidence and trust in their pupils. Being rigorous involves ratcheting the learning up a notch. It calls for students to be slightly better writers, to think at a higher level, or to demonstrate the ability to discover concepts on their own. The high level of expectations for their students' learning and success separates exceptional teachers from the rest. Rigorous teachers simply never settle for pretty good. They approach every lesson, and each and every student, as a challenge to grow toward excellence.

I knew a teacher who set extremely high standards for his students. To him it was never a question of students not being able to succeed; it was always a question of how far he could take them. He taught calculus and physics and observing his classes was a real joy. More than simply teaching concepts or theories, he taught students how to think. A fifteen-minute lecture on some law of the universe was presented as a series of questions and thought patterns that led students to a complete and thorough understanding of the law. It was hard stuff, but this teacher made it appear easy. In every school where I have worked, graduates have come back after experiencing college work to praise the high school teachers who had provided rigorous learning experiences. The students also mention that these teachers found ways to support them through the rigorous coursework. These teachers know that rigor does not mean piling on more work. College admissions personnel report that a rigorous high school course of study successfully completed becomes the best predictor of a student's college success. I contend that teachers have a responsibility to make academic rigor accessible to each student, not just those who were identified as gifted and talent in third grade. We know that high expectations are a key component of quality schooling for every student.

4. Be **R**espectful

In chapter 3, I talked about how important it is that teachers never raise their voice, argue with a child, or be disrespectful towards them. Nothing can derail a student's educational experience faster than being disrespected by an adult. Respecting students is such a simple tenant for success, yet such a difficult one to live up to. When all is said and done, the teachers that are most respected are the ones who show students the most respect. The teachers who seem to have a level of understanding, empathy, and acceptance for their students are the ones students gravitate to. Teachers who rarely have classroom management issues are probably in that enviable position because they have figured out how not to back students into corners.

Being respectful really begins by adhering to the golden rule. If we treat others as we wish to be treated, our work is nearly done. Occasionally, we have to invoke another standard rule, such as turning the other cheek or counting to ten when students test our patience, but life typically gives us what we give to others. When we have the students' respect, the job of teacher or administrator becomes so much easier. We earn respect by giving it.

5. Be **R**esponsive

One of the quickest ways to lose the confidence of others is to not be responsive to their needs. Failure to respond to a parent's request can be devastating to a teacher, and a reputation of unresponsiveness can often affect an entire school. I become incensed when one of my teachers does not reply to e-mail or voice mail messages because I believe those failures taint all of our work. Our staff could effectively respond to 30 or 40 parental communications and no one would notice. But the one communication that is dropped is the one that circulates around town. The dropped communication is the one that triggers negative comments about teachers: that they work 7.5-hour days, have summers off, or only teach kids xxx-number of minutes per day.

The same can be said for returning tests and quizzes on time or keeping promises to students. Educators have to understand that we shoot ourselves in the foot when we are not responsive to our students or their parents. We work in a service industry and we need to be mindful of the expectations that others have of us. When my dad was a patient on a cancer ward, my family had expectations for the nurses and doctors who provided care. Nothing was more important to us than his comfort, yet we could do little in that regard without responsive caretakers. Educators, teachers, and administrators alike are entrusted with the children of loving parents who also demand and deserve their responsiveness. Schools exist, not for teachers but for the pupils they teach and, as important as being responsive to parents can be, responding to the students is even more important.

6. Have Routines

Teachers have to have a plan for how they are going to run their classroom. They have to establish routines that are consistent and dependable in order for their teaching to be effective. Great content and great teaching strategies are often wasted in a classroom where routines have not been established. Classroom management, classroom rules, behavior plans, transitions schemes, and utilization of space all affect the learning of students. Routines are one of the twelve Rs because they are an essential part of the work of teachers. As I mentioned earlier, I once heard a conference presenter indicate that the most important word in classroom management had only two letters: N-O, and the trick was to say the word with love. Having routines is a bit more complicated than that, but not by much. Students need to understand the expectations, be familiar with the structure, and experience consistency in their classrooms. Having strong routines serves two purposes: it allows for student success, and it helps make teacher survival possible. I marvel at how hard the first year of teaching is. In fact, even veteran teachers moving to a new school experience a difficult transition year. The second year at a school for both new and experienced teachers is like night and day compared to the first year. Most of this has to do with the difficulty of establishing routines, either because of inexperience or being in new surroundings. Carefully thought-out routines are a vital part of great teaching.

7. Be a **R**ole Model

So much has already been said about the interpersonal aspect of teaching. Throughout this book, I have hinted that teaching is not about having students know what we know, think like we think, or like what we like. It is more about helping them find themselves, to become relevant. What has not yet been said discussed is the importance of setting examples for our students. The fact that students watch what we do and that our behavior affects them more than what we say, is really at the heart of this tenet. If we want students to be ethical, then we must model that. If we want students to be respectful, we must show them how. If we want students to display a tireless work ethic or be reflective about their work, we need to show them how that is done. We do not need a detailed road map to be a good role model; we simply need to be introspective. All we have to do is apply the golden rule to our efforts. I cannot count the number of times I have seen educators act in ways that they would never accept from a student in their classroom. They might be negative in a meeting, hurtful to a colleague, sloppy in their work, or tardy to school. These same teachers often turn around and are intolerant of adolescent mistakes. We can expect and receive so much more from our students if we first model what we need from them. We know that students will strive to replicate what their teachers do. Let us hope that we can, on our worst days, be worthy of their imitation.

8. **R**est and Relax

In every one of the eight school systems I which I have worked, there have been teachers who hovered on the edge of an emotional breakdown. Every event led them to push the panic button and nothing they had on their plate ever appeared easy. My hunch is that you have had the same experience in the places you have worked; perhaps this observation holds true for all work forces, regardless of occupation. Yet, for every one of these harried colleagues, I have known four or five who go through their daily teaching routine like the man on the trapeze: with the greatest of ease. How can this be? How can the same job requirements create high levels of stress for some and not for others? Obviously the difference in people would account for some of this, but not all. Much of the difference between those teachers who handle the job

in an effortless manner and those who seem to be paddling upstream lies in the areas of planning and organization. Effective teachers plan daily, practice strategies and routines that maximize student engagement and minimize management issues, and commit to the work.

Yet, there is more. Teachers who are not overwhelmed by their jobs have a lifestyle that allows for rest and relaxation. I know a teacher who never seems to break a sweat at work. He does an excellent job teaching, coaches several sports, is a friendly colleague to others, is always there for a student in need, and goes home to a busy family life with three small children. Somehow he glides through the day looking centered and balanced. He exercises regularly, has interests outside of school, and is able, on most days, to leave work at work. The lesson provided by this teacher is a simple one. Allowing for rest and relaxation provides us with the energy to succeed at work, while avoiding the trap of being over-consumed by job-related stress. Following this teacher's example is simply a matter of choice. We can form the habit of getting regular exercise, cultivate outside interests and hobbies, and ensure that we get enough sleep and good nutrition. Success in these areas requires us to consciously work to avoid the trap of letting our jobs consume us. All of this is easier to accomplish when we are offered onsite wellness programs, or join others in a supportive network to live a balanced life.

9. Be Responsible

Whenever teachers are polled regarding what would give them better working conditions, invariably they wish for higher levels of student responsibility. If only our students took more responsibility for their learning. If only students acted more responsibly, the work of teaching would be considerably more enjoyable. As a long-time school administrator, I echo that cry when I am asked what I think would make my job easier. Wouldn't it be nice if students could act more responsibly? Absolutely, but the road leading toward greater student responsibility is paved by the modeling of our teachers. We can demand and expect more responsibility from our students when our staff delivers the same.

What does it really mean to be a responsible employee or a responsible member of a school community? At the top of my list would be delivering on promises and living up to organizational expectations. An example of the former would be to correct student work in a thoughtful and timely manner. Teachers who procrastinate on returning corrected work model irresponsibility and invite the same from their students. In terms of meeting organizational standards, we only need to note which teachers are always late posting grades or frequently arrive late to school or to their duty stations. It amazes me how often these same teachers have zero tolerance for student tardiness or procrastination.

Part of the deal about being a teacher includes a certain level of responsibility that cannot be questioned by our customers: students and parents. If I could ever supervise a staff that was totally responsible, we would redefine the meaning of an effective school. I am continually amazed at how effective schools actually are, given the fact that every faculty I have ever worked with has a small but significant percentage of teachers who act irresponsibly. The workings of schools are complex and varied. How nice it would be, how much easier it would become, if everyone assumed their share of responsibility. So much of my energy over the years has been spent helping my school recover event after event, deadline after deadline, from the irresponsibility of a minority of our teaching staff. Teachers need to set personal goals to meet deadlines and fulfill teaching responsibilities for the sake of organizational success. Think of the time saved and efficiency realized if this came to be. Think of how this would affect each student's level of responsibility.

10. Reach for the Stars

Although this "R" might seem redundant if you consider reaching for the stars as just another way to express the need for rigor and high expectations, it represents more than that. It involves focusing on dreams and possibilities for our students and for ourselves. If we are just getting started, the sky is the limit. People often make the mistaken assumption that rigor and high expectations are a result of more or harder work. The idea that harder work leads to rigor or higher expectations may have merit, but more work often defeats our goals and becomes just more of the same and leads to busy work. In order to avoid confusion between rigor and reaching for the stars, think of the idea of cultivating student dreams. In education there exists a whole series of balancing acts. Teachers must learn to consider the equilibrium between inspiration and control and how to deal with the needs of the individual versus the needs of the classroom. Excellence in teaching also requires us to manage the balance between the refinement and realization of students' dreams and their overall academic success.

We received a note from the parent of one of our seniors that brought a smile to my face. The parent was thrilled that her son had completed his requirements to achieve an early graduation and was set to go to a culinary arts school at semester's end. The note described the wonderful support this student had received from our school community and how the boy would someday invite all of us to his restaurant. The parent explained that all of this was possible because our staff had balanced the reality of her child's struggles with learning with the dream he held to one day become a chef. We never gave the student the message that he could not become a chef, that he could not realize his dream, but we also never let him dream of the future without the realization that he had to face up to the present and fulfill his responsibilities as a student.

11. Be Resilient

Even though I have worked in schools for thirty-seven years, I still find each day to be somewhat unpredictable. As much as schools are places of unpredictability, we can always bet that some things will occur on a regular basis. Stuff happens. Don't you feel, although it cannot be proved scientifically, that student misbehavior increases during a full moon? Do you sense that on the days following Halloween, students are a bit more hyperactive from all the sugar? The minute it starts spitting snow, students are going to start fidgeting in anticipation of an early dismissal. And doesn't Murphy's Law—if something can go wrong it probably will—seem to kick in at the most inopportune times? These have all been the case with me. If we consider that resiliency can be defined as our ability to recover rapidly from illness, change, or misfortune. Or perhaps the ability of something to regain its shape after being bent, stretched, or compressed, we can understand its relevance to the teaching profession. How we respond to the unexpected, how we respond to stress, or how we respond to the tensions of our daily work with students in many ways defines how successful we will be at reaching our goals.

Al Siebert, author of *The Resiliency Advantage*, suggests that resilience is essential in today's world. He claims that, "In today's workplace everyone feels pressure to get more done, of higher quality, with fewer people, in less time, with less money. In our personal lives things are changing so rapidly everyone must learn to be change proficient, cope with unexpected setbacks and overcome unwanted adversities."[2] Does this sound like the perfect description of our job and daily experiences in teaching? The good news is that resiliency can be learned, practiced, and developed over time.

Siebert contends that all of us are born with the potential to increase our resiliency and lists five graduated levels of resiliency. The first addresses the need to maintain health and stability and having the energy to fully function. The second level involves our ability to cope with outward challenges that require strong problem-solving skills. The next level focuses on the inner self, such as processing a strong self-esteem. Fourthly, Seibert discusses the attributes and skills found in resilient people. Finally, the highest level of resiliency is the ability to turn misfortune into good fortune. He calls this a "talent for serendipity,"[3] or how I often hear of people making lemonade

---

[2]Retrieved from www.resiliencycenter.com
[3]Siebert, Al. *The Resiliency Advantage: Master change, Thrive Under Pressure and Bounce from Setbacks*, Practical Psychology Press, 2005. p. 9.

out of lemons. The most applicable information for teaching that Siebert's work offers me is the reminder that when we are faced with adversity:

- We can create either barriers or bridges to a better future.
- We can learn to build up our own innate abilities to become resilient.
- We can, in our struggle to recover from adverse situations, develop abilities we did not know we possessed.

These points paint a hopeful and worthy portrait of the potential of resilient educators. We have the awesome opportunity and responsibility to model resilience for the children we teach. We are continually faced with choices regarding how we react to situations. We can allow experiences to build us up or to diminish us, and if we earnestly seek the former, we can truly amaze ourselves. Is there a dazzlingly resilient teacher looking back at you when you look in a mirror? There could be!

12. Teaching as its own Reward

Arthur Ashe once said, "From what we get, we can make a living. What we give, however, makes a life." Make no mistake about it; people who enter the teaching profession should be looking at creating a life because it is certainly not the easiest way to make a living. Long before we decided to become a teacher, we probably decided that driving a Lexus or owning a vacation home on the ocean were not things that would become part of our long-range plans. However, choosing to teach offers other advantages that are not represented by high salaries or material gains. We have heard some of the clichés, such as "To teach is to touch the future," or "Teaching allows you to stay young." From my experiences, these are very real benefits associated with teaching. We do get to stay involved with the excitement associated with youth, and we do get to help shape the next generation of adults. There are many rewards that, with the right mindset, can minimize the disappointment we might feel driving around in a beat-up Honda Civic.

According to the 1958 writings of Fredrick Hertzberg on motivational theory, items such as wages and benefits are not the motivators people think they are. We should focus more on growth, learning, challenge, and success to motivate people over the long haul. Hertzberg cites that achievement, recognition, and the work itself are factors that lead to extreme job satisfaction.[4] This has certainly been my experience with teaching. The joy of my work has never been the excitement of a paycheck. Instead, I am deeply inspired and motivated by the achievement of my students, the recognition they receive, and the times that their recognition comes back to me in the form of a thank-you note from the parents or a smile from the student. The work environment is equally appealing. I love the events that occur around a school. Drama, sports, dances, and the social scene go a long way toward offsetting the countless meetings and other drudgeries I do not enjoy.

When speaking to pre-service educators about the advantages of teaching, I am quick to point out how lucky I feel to be in education, even though I possibly could have been much richer had I entered the private sector. "Possibly" is an important word in the preceding sentence because two of the things that teaching has provided me with have been stability and predictability. The private sector might not have yielded the same certainty or stability. My wife and I are both teachers and we have been able to live contentedly, raise a family, and prepare for a comfortable, although certainly not elaborate, retirement. We benefited a great deal as our children went through school. We were there with them, saw them more than most parents saw their children and shared vacation time and summers together. I believe teaching is a great way to make a life. I am very excited when one of my former students decides that teaching might be for them. We need more people who enjoyed school to come back and teach. Wouldn't it be wonderful if all of our teachers could have enjoyed school? Imagine the experiences students would have if that were the case.

I might lead a parade demanding higher salaries for our teachers, but I am not bitter about my choice to teach or my financial condition because of it. I have always had food on the table, a good health insurance plan—benefits that 50% of the people in

---

[4]Herzberg, Fredrick, B. Mausner, and B. Bloch Snijdermen (1959). *The Motivation to Work*. New York.

my community would love to have—and best of all, I get to work each day in an environment where I can make a difference.

In a moment of weakness, you might hear me wish I was independently wealthy, but ten days out of ten, I am proud of what I do. If I could not say that, I would not be of much value to my school or my students. Educators need to be proud of who they are and what they accomplish. One of the prerequisites for being a teacher should be to never feel that we have settled for something unimportant or less that we might have had otherwise.

Comparing our experiences as teachers with the twelve professional standards that have been outlined in this chapter is an exercise that all teachers should do. In order to create a school for each student, we have to be sure that our teachers are approaching all of these important areas effectively. By doing so, we provide our schools with the possibility of helping students find these same qualities and high standards within themselves.

Joining a Team

The world is changing at an alarming pace and that is certainly the case with teaching as well. What was true 30 years ago bears little or no resemblance to what is true today. For example, in my first teaching position, I had an assignment that was equal to a job that now takes three staff people to handle. Expectations and the speed of life have changed so much that teachers seem to have all that they can handle with their responsibilities. I remember completing my job thirty years ago with energy to spare. Perhaps I have selective memory, but I think there is something to be said about how busy everyone is today. If you are a teaching veteran with 25 or more years of experience under your belt, you probably remember sitting in the teacher's room reading a newspaper during your preparation time. You probably can recall sitting in that room and hearing hunting and fishing stories, exchanging recipes, or participating in a heated political debate. I am certain that you also recall some times when there were educational benefits that occurred in this setting. Somehow there just seemed to be more time; I cannot imagine reading the newspaper now during breaks. There used to be more time to catch our breath, to escape from being "on" every second of the day, and more time to forge collegial friendships with our peers.

Although there are many benefits to the changes that have occurred in the dwindling use of teachers' rooms (they could also be very negative places), the collegial piece has been a terrible loss. The nature of our work requires that we have solid support systems, people who share our burdens and experiences and are able to support and encourage us on a daily basis. Modern-day schools are far different from what they were two or three decades ago and consequently, the social aspect of teaching has also changed. Faculties were often a close-knit family of people who socialized outside of school. My early recollections of teaching involve strong memories of friendships I forged with other teachers and how that added a pleasing dimension to the job that seems to be missing today. In my current school, one of our teachers hosts a holiday social every year and though it is a wonderful event, the majority of attendees are the older teachers, and even retired teachers. At these gatherings, we hear a lot of conversation about the "good old days" and how things were different back then. We hear about how the faculty was closer knit and more involved in each other's lives outside of school. People were part of a larger network of friendship and support.

There are some exceptions to this that are worthy of mention. The guidance staff at my current school eats lunch together every day in the guidance reception area. The office is open for business, but they all sit around a huge table and eat together. During this thirty-minute time frame, they rarely talk business. They talk instead about weddings, movies, books, and current events. Our guidance chair often talks about the fact that if we are going to be there for our students, we have to be healthy as a faculty. He mentions these staff lunches often to other teachers in hopes that the idea might catch on. Several weeks ago, a math teacher relayed to me how much fun she was having this year at school, how her attitude was different than in previous years. She attributed this to the fact that she had started joining the rest of the math teachers for lunch. We also have a group of four younger teachers who share a 30-minute commute to school. This common time to be with people and share experiences is good for the soul. I also think it provides an excellent example for our students. If they see teachers forging friendships and caring for one another, then students are more likely to do the same.

The more we can find ways to build a friendly and supportive atmosphere among ourselves, the more rewarding and satisfying our work will be. While this seemed to happen almost instinctively when I started teaching, people today have to make a conscious effort to forge these relationships in and out of school. But do not give up when it proves to be challenging. Joining with people who have common experiences is well worth the effort. It provides another reason to get up every morning and go to a job that you love.

Chapter 5: Discussion Questions

1. In considering the 12 Rs, are there any that are more important than others? Which would you consider your strongest area? Your weakest?
2. Is there a need for educators to address the realities around the accountability and responsibilities of teachers? How could this be structured to promote positive discussions?
3. What are some of the benefits and incentives that teachers could derive from the effort to move towards a "school for each student" approach?
4. What implications does the following quote by Henry David Thoreau have for your work in school reform? "Things do not change, people do."
5. What would we need to do to make school more about students and less about organizational needs?
6. Can you think of other groups or places in your life that offer a strong support system? How are they successful? Can you think of ways to incorporate what is working from these other groups into your school relationships?

Chapter 6

A Wider Perspective

"Freedom to think differently—can be society's most precious gift to itself. The first duty of a school is to defend and cherish it."

—Arthur Bestor

In order to create successful educational programs, we have to look beyond the walls of the classroom to see that school is a part of a larger tapestry, one that includes economic, social, and political influences. If we ignore the significance of these influences, success will be hard to come by. Teachers have to be aware of the pressures that affect their work and the lives of their students.

This chapter will investigate the change process, systems thinking, and the social and political structures that impact what can be accomplished in schools. The awareness that these pressures exist and that we must actively manage their influence on our job provides a mandate for us to connect our work to a bigger picture. This book is about channeling our work to better meet the needs of each individual student, about doing whatever it takes to help students succeed. But this can only happen if we can first see the big picture.

The Snake Was Wrong

It is extremely easy for educators to lose sight of their objectives in a society and political climate that is so committed to winning. One of the easiest paths for a teacher to travel is the one that leads to the top for a small segment of their students. The path that leads to higher SAT scores, Advance Placement or International Baccalaureate success, National Honor Society inductions and the acceptance of a few students to prestigious colleges. These lofty goals are definitely part of our educational mission, but not at the exclusion of other students and other programs. We must find ways to avoid getting trapped in the rat race of higher test scores and elitism. Central to our mission is the responsibility we have for each student, not just a select few. The responsibility we have to help all of them to become somebody, to become relevant. The following spoof of a familiar biblical story illustrates how distorted priorities can become. I do not know where or when I happened upon this parody and therefore cannot provide an appropriate citation. The parody cleverly explores the tension between having fun and keeping score, but it could just as easily be about chasing high test scores and creating a climate where learning is intrinsic as opposed to extrinsic.

In the Beginning

In the beginning, God didn't make just two people; he made a bunch of us because he wanted us to have a lot of fun. And he said you can't really have fun unless there is a whole gang of you. He put us in Eden, which was a combination garden and playground and park and told us to have fun. At first we did have fun just like he expected; we rolled down the hills, waded in the streams, climbed on the tress, swung on the vines, ran in the woods, hid in the forest, and acted silly. We laughed a lot. Then one day, the snake told us that we weren't having real fun because we weren't keeping score. Back then we didn't know what score was. When he explained it, we still couldn't see the fun, but he said we should give an apple to the person who was best at all the games and we'd never know who the best was without keeping score. We could all see the fun of that, of course, because we were all sure that we were the best.

It was different after that; we yelled a lot and we had to make up new scoring rules for most of the games. Other games like frolicking we stopped playing because they were too hard to score. By the time God found out what had happened, we were spending about 45 minutes a day actually playing and the rest of the time working out scoring. God was wrath about that, very, very wrath. He said we couldn't use his garden anymore because we weren't having fun. We told him we were having lots of fun, he was just being narrow-minded because it wasn't exactly the kind of fun he originally thought of. He wouldn't listen; he kicked us out. And he said we couldn't come back until we stopped keeping score. To rub it in, to get our attention, he said that we were all going to die and our scores wouldn't mean anything anyway. He was wrong. My cumulative game score is now 16.548, and that means a lot to me. If I can raise it to 20,000 before I die, I'll know I've accomplished something. Even if I can't, my life has a great deal of meaning because I taught my children to score high and they'll be able to reach 20,000 or even 30,000. Really, it was life in the garden that didn't mean anything. Fun is great in its place, but without scoring, there is no reason for it. God actually has a very superficial view of life and I am certainly glad my children are being raised away from his influence. We are lucky! We're all very grateful to the snake.

In this satire, the people sold out to the temptation of keeping score. In schools, educators face the temptation of selling out to the race for excellence. I have been in eight schools and each did an admirable job with the top tiers of their student population. We did good work with the students who had parents that were connected to the school and valued education. Students who had high aspirations and were socially connected received quality programming. Interestingly, these schools also provided sound programming and support for their special education students. What seemed to be missing in all eight of the districts where I worked was the appropriate focus on the students in the middle. If we take into consideration how societal and political pressures operate, this is not a surprising finding. Affluent parents put pressure on school systems for gifted and talented programs. They keep up a continuous physical and financial presence in the school, which causes a spotlight to shine on their students. On the opposite end of the spectrum, students with disabilities or learning differences have strong advocacy groups and parental involvement to push for special services.

Abandoned in the middle are students who fall off the radar screen. Only marginal efforts are expended here because they are not the "squeaky wheels." They show up, do not cause disturbances, and are largely forgotten. This may not be a universal condition, but the implications are painfully clear.

Successful schools need to resist the temptation and, in fact, push back against the pressures to marginalize "average" students in order to chase test scores, or to lavish attention on the squeakiest wheels. Learning, or more accurately, the love of learning is what is truly important. We need to guard against losing our soul in the chase for extrinsic rewards. I am not suggesting that this is an easy thing to do; the pressures to sell out are incredible. What I am suggesting is that we watch out for snakes and keep each student on our radar screen.

Change and Change Again

A reality that goes with teaching, as it does with life, is that change is inevitable. In Spencer Johnson's bestseller entitled, *Who Moved My Cheese*, he tells his readers to embrace change because, like it or not, it is going to happen. Schools as organizations have earned a reputation for being resistant to change, and many contend that schools are essentially the same today as they were in the 1950s. That reputation is certainly a tension point for leaders trying to advance school reform and improve school systems, but it has little to do with the reality of being an educator. Regardless of the rigidity of the schools we work in, we must change day-by-day, minute-by-minute. The ability to adapt to change, or "to savor the new cheese," as Johnson's metaphor suggests, is at the heart of building a school for each student. Without some effort spent on developing resiliency skills in the midst of a constantly changing environment, working toward this mission will be quite a challenge.

Imagine how hard it would be to go to work every day, unable to adjust to the day-to-day variations that students provide us with? There are many teachers in our schools whose abilities are diminished because they cannot adapt to change. Through my many years of education, I have been one of those people who enjoy the process of change. Philip Schlecty, the author of *Inventing Better Schools*, would probably label me a pioneer: a person who seemingly never met an idea that they did not like. Change is difficult for everybody, including pioneers. Even though I have been a change agent, in each place that I have worked, I have also encountered changes that I did not relish. I might have played a huge role in changing hundreds of things in the organizations where I have worked, but there have been times when I acted more like a saboteur than a pioneer. Schlecty advances the idea that those teachers who block new ideas are often the same ones who, earlier in their careers, were pioneers. He suggests that somewhere along the way, they were disappointed after investing passionately in a failed change effort and are no longer as willing to devote themselves to change.[1] This has huge implications for whether or not we will be successful in our efforts to change the climate of a school from an all-student mentality. I suspect that many of the teachers who need to jump on board in order to create a school for each student might be in this category. They may have the necessary beliefs, but have grown exhausted by the effort required to put those beliefs into practice.

My superintendent returned from a conference and shared a handout from a session he attended presented by Terry B. Grice on *Leading for Results*. The handout listed twelve harsh realities related to change. One in particular that he highlights is the fact that "individuals opt to be victims of change rather than advocates of change." I contend that this is a real challenge that teachers face. They can either expend their energy pushing against pending changes or they can get out front and lead the parade. Although an oversimplification, this is an area of potential joy or potential suffering. I have seen many teachers who spend much of their time being miserable due to the change initiatives swirling around them. They are suspicious of whoever is promoting the change and have little interest in discovering whether or not the idea holds any merit. Consequently, they spend their valuable and limited energy in conflict with the change, rather than making a contribution to the change. Following is one example.

> Rose was a great homeroom teacher. She had been a great homeroom teacher for years. Along the way, she had developed exceptional skills. She took quick and accurate attendance, had developed shortcuts to help keep her 20 or so students organized, and had found ways to really connect with the students in the 10 minutes she had with them each morning. In her twentieth year at Park Middle School, a movement was initiated to create an advisory program that would replace the traditional homeroom model. The proponents of the new program felt that the shift would improve student achievement, serve to connect

---

[1] Schlechty, Philip. "On the Frontier of School Reform with Trailblazers, Pioneers and Settlers." *Journal of Staff Development* 14, (Fall 1993), 14:46–51.

students with a meaningful adult, and provide the school with a better organizational structure. Rose was not very excited about this idea. In fact, she spoke out against it every chance she got. She would tell anyone who wanted to listen that the new program was not necessary. She used the "if it ain't broke why fix it?" argument and was quite a blocker in the eyes of her colleagues who were promoting the program. They could not understand why a teacher of her skills and ability would be so negative. Wasn't this about a program that had the potential to be so good for students? It was not like her to disagree with something that was good for students. They were even more confused about the fact that Rose's successful homeroom practices were at the heart of their vision for what the new Advisory program would look like. So why was she so opposed?

There were three things at the center of Rose's hesitation. First, she had a very successful homeroom, so it was very hard for her to see any compelling reason to change. In order for change to be embraced, a person must see a justification for it and in her view, homeroom was working just fine the way it was. Second, Rose felt a sense of loss due to the pending start of an Advisory program. She had forged strong relationships with her homeroom and did not want to abandon those associations in order to experiment with the unknowns of a new idea. Finally, she felt that her competencies were being challenged. She was the world's greatest homeroom teacher. Why would she venture off on a new concept where her skills were undeveloped?

For nearly a year, the staff at Park Middle School tugged and pulled at the idea of instituting an advisory program. Finally, the idea became a reality and the school abandoned homerooms and restructured around advisories. In the end, mostly because Rose was such a quality teacher, she did become a successful advisor. What if this story could have had a little different twist? What if Rose had been at the front of the parade? What if the people who had promoted the idea of advisories had helped Rose feel like she had the skill set needed to create the model they were aiming for? What if Rose could have been convinced that this program could offer every student at her school the relationships and environment that she had created in her homeroom? All of these "what ifs" suggest dual responsibility for changing the outcome of this story. Rose could have taken more responsibility for being at the heart of the process of looking at a new program rather than reacting to forces imposed from the outside. The people proposing the change also had a responsibility for bringing Rose into the discussion. Either approach would have brought her valuable skills into the equation.

Even though we could go on and on about many different aspects of change, I want to make sure that we cover a few key points. The fact that change is inevitable is one point. I would also offer the idea that if you want to be content in your role as a teacher, maintaining the status quo is probably not the route I would encourage you to take. Teaching and learning is a dynamic, open experience that requires a great deal of flexibility and resiliency. We need to go into this work understanding that change is going to happen, and commit ourselves to acquiring the skills we need in order to be able to change gracefully. It is about being proactive rather than reactive in our work.

If change is inevitable, regardless of what we do, then why would we not make an effort to impact our environment as educators as much as possible by getting involved? I think that a person experiences a much different feeling when they are involved in a process than when they are falling victim to it. Considering that our students mimic our actions, what should we model about change?

I have chosen the serenity prayer as a fitting way to conclude our brief examination of the changes that all teachers will encounter. Within this prayer are embedded three skills that are essential in order to thrive in an educational environment. Wisdom, courage, and serenity need to be in every teacher's tool kit.

"God grant me the serenity to accept the things I cannot change . . .
The courage to change the things I can . . .
And the wisdom to know the difference."

Work from a Context

Several years ago, a student, as part of his committee work on exploring alternative ideas for school governance, summarized the following five types of decision-making:

1. **Policy/Precedent Based**. Decisions that are covered in school board policy, are based on strong precedents, or are a matter of law.
2. **Isolated**. Decisions that are made that afford little or no time for collaboration. An example would be responding to a safety threat.
3. **Contextual**. Decisions based on data or fact-finding.
4. **Democratic**. Decisions that are reached through voting or consensus-building.
5. **Wise/Inspired**. Decisions that are made because they simply should not be denied.

As teachers who must make countless decisions on a daily, even hourly, basis, it would be wise to have a thorough understanding of what drives the decisions we make. This student captured five types of decision-making quite well. The first two types of decisions are not difficult to make, such as laws and procedures that do not have shades of gray. They are mostly black and white and require little interpretation. If state law requires that we report any cases of suspected child abuse to our principal or state protective service agency, we have no choice in the matter. If a student falls on the playground and appears to have lost consciousness, we do not have the luxury of looking in a policy book or gathering other opinions, we dial 9-1-1.

However, many of the decisions that teachers face are not to be found in these categories. Most of our decisions fall in the third and fourth categories: contextual and democratic. This is where the teacher has latitude, where there is the luxury of time and flexibility associated with choice. There is also less structure, so more responsibility falls on the teacher to rely on their experience, context, relationship- and rapport-building, and wisdom when making these types of decisions.

Educators need to get better at making contextual decisions, decisions that are based on quantitative and qualitative data. In order to defend and justify decisions, teachers need to be able to clearly articulate the context surrounding their choice. If extensive research or data indicates that high school students perform better on testing during mid-morning hours, then pushing for a mid-morning testing time would be defensible. If unwanted lunchroom behaviors began to show up after the cafeteria becomes overcrowded, it would make sense to limit the number of students entering the cafeteria. Although these are straightforward examples, schools and classrooms do not always operate in this manner. More attention needs to be paid to the framework or circumstances that might impact decisions. Paying attention to data, survey results, or the opinion of others all serve to influence decisions in a positive way. People who are not very good at gathering and utilizing pertinent information often find themselves on the defensive. In contrast are those who can clearly explain the context of their decisions and rarely face harsh questioning. Decisions made in context are thoughtful, and thoughtfulness generally begets thoughtfulness.

Schools and classrooms can also provide a haven for the democratic process; a place where public discourse leads a group to a shared decision. This is an area where educators need to assume more responsibility. Teachers who allow students a share in the decision-making process not only teach them valuable citizenship skills, they also increase the likelihood that students will support whatever decision is reached. Without a doubt, this involves more work. No one ever said that democracy was easy, but I, for one, believe it is a much healthier way to make decisions.

Occasionally, teachers make a decision because it is simply the right thing to do. These are the decisions that are wise or inspired. Decisions that make so much sense that to not make them would be a mistake. For example, a student is late turning in an assignment, which usually means an automatic grade reduction, and the teacher discovers that the student's grandfather passed away two days earlier. An inspired decision would be to not penalize that student in this instance. Another example would be to allow a student who is interested in early childhood education to do an apprenticeship at a daycare for a senior project. It just makes sense, so we work through whatever obstacles arise and make it happen.

I believe that teacher job satisfaction and success is directly related to the method of decision-making they employ. If they spend a majority of their time in the mode of controlling, legislating, and dictating, I fear that they will experience sadness and frustration in their job. If teachers can make a majority of their decisions in context or through democratic practices, I predict a more joyful outcome. And finally, on those occasions when decisions are made with courageous inspiration, outcomes can be wonderful! Moving toward a school for each student starts with inspiration. It involves building a case for it though data collection and research. Then it involves helping bring others to our way of thinking by modeling professionalism through consistent practice of the twelve tenets of great teaching.

Finding Our Way

I was speaking to a group of eighth-grade teachers one January about their students' transition into high school. We were attempting to start the course selection procedure earlier than in past years to allow more time to thoughtfully complete the process. I received some unexpected resistance from the middle school staff as I proposed an earlier start on creating ninth-grade schedules. Eventually, one of the teachers shared what was behind the concern and resistance. Some staff at the middle school felt that once their students received their high school schedule, they would stop working in their eighth-grade classrooms. I was rendered speechless as thoughts of eighth graders having senioritis swirled through my head. I remember thinking that education is in a lot of trouble if the only way we can get students to work in middle school is by dangling the carrot of high school placement. Yet, I should be careful about judging, because much of what happens in high school is driven by the quest for college admission. In the heat of that moment, I wish that I had remembered Dorothy De Zouche's quote, "If I were asked to enumerate ten educational stupidities, the giving of grades would head the list. . . . If I can't give a child a better reason for studying than a grade on a report card, I ought to lock my desk and go home and stay there."

Our educational compass for student motivation has to revolve around the intrinsic value of learning and the excitement of discovery. It cannot be about numbers, about keeping score. Are we on course?

Closely related to whether or not we have lost our way, schools and colleges throughout the country struggle with what seems to be an epidemic of cheating and plagiarism. Are there some compelling reasons for this or are today's youth simply unethical? I believe that there is more than enough blame to go around regarding the issue of academic dishonesty in our schools. We could start with grade grubbing and the pressure on students to excel, and the competitive edge needed to gain admission to first-choice schools. We could then move on to the strain that students feel about juggling multiple priorities, such as sports, jobs, and social pressures. Let us not forget the hours of homework, some of which is nothing more than busy work that is required of students under the guise of rigor. And then there is the Internet, with its easy access to words, ideas, papers, and answers. Throw in the models of dishonesty provide by the adults in their lives and I have to wonder why cheating is not even more prevalent.

I become very discouraged when I hear an educator spouting off that the cure for academic dishonesty should be stiffer consequences. I immediately conclude that the educator simply cannot see the symptoms behind the acts of academic dishonesty. I believe teachers have a responsibility to not be so quick to categorize cheating as a character flaw. Certainly, in some instances they would be right, but I doubt if everyone who ever copied an answer, did not cite a source properly, or made up an excuse about a missing homework assignment has a flawed character. Teachers need to protect young people from themselves because developmentally, they may not be able to align their impulsive actions with consequences. Too many teachers simply pretend cheating does not happen and then harshly deal with the student when it "surprisingly" does. I applaud teachers who painstakingly work to create plagiarism-proof assignments or work tirelessly to help students learn to paraphrase and correctly cite sources. I think teachers should rearrange their rooms or create multiple variations of a test to create fewer opportunities for cheating during exams. I encourage teachers to carefully explain their expectations about honesty in collaborative learning situations. I believe that these extra efforts show the student that the teacher cares deeply about their academic safety. It repeatedly reinforces with students that cheating is unacceptable and that their teacher is going the extra mile to see that it does not happen to them. The best weapon against dishonesty is modeling that it is unacceptable by what we do to prevent it.

When it does happen, when a student does cheat, it needs to be dealt with forcefully. Students should receive a zero for the assignment, parents should be called, and the student should meet with the principal. It is also very effective to make the student responsible for telling their parents what happened. Students need to experience discomfort and embarrassment in order to make a different choice in the future. But, for some educators, and I say this with sadness, punishment and shame have replaced educational counseling.

Students must also be given a chance to undo the mess they created. I heard a high-powered Ph.D. candidate talk about a life-altering cheating incident that occurred in her freshmen year of high school. The school administration had her speak to every advisory group in the school about her mistake during the fall of her sophomore year. She claimed that since that incident, cheating has never again entered her mind. She remarked that the consequence of speaking to others about her poor choice was far more effective than changing her grade.

We need to be extremely careful about the emphasis we put on grading and all that goes with that. The school for each student model would insulate students from some of the academic dishonesty issues that exist in schools by reducing the amount of competition between students. Finding our way past the surface issues and helping students develop academic and ethical skills are all part of our job as teachers.

Successful teachers can empathize with their students and the pressures they face, work to protect them from themselves, and provide opportunities for students to recover and grow from their mistakes.

Choose Your Attitude

Four or five years ago, I discovered a world-renowned customer satisfaction program used in the business sector called the FISH! Philosophy.[2] This program that has its roots in a successful fish market in Seattle. It proposes a way of serving customers that leads to high profits and employee satisfaction. Including its tenets in a book about redirecting the mission of America's schools is most appropriate. In fact, it serves as a summary of the points made about creating a school for each student. Pike's Place Fish Market claims to be world-famous because they adhere to four beliefs about successful customer service. Let us see what these are and how we might apply their philosophy to our goad of truly personalizing our schools.

FISH!

The fishmongers bring a component of play into their daily work. They joke with patrons, toss fish around in a game-like fashion in order to entertain customers, and do nothing that hints of boredom. Everything is aimed at having fun at work, but they also manage to sell an incredible amount of fish. As teachers, can we create a fun, playful environment in our classrooms? Can we joke with our students, make fun of ourselves, and bring a touch of lightheartedness to learning? And if we did, is it possible that our students could be more engaged and perhaps learn more? I believe that the answer to all of these questions is an emphatic "yes." Classrooms need to be places of laughter rather than places of gloom, disinterest, and intimidation. Students need to be like wide-eyed youngsters at a circus, on the edge of their seats wondering what wonderful thing will happen next. We should not put too much emphasis on the hard work associated with achievement. Schools should be places of play, where hard work can be fun. I believe we have the ability to accomplish this.

---

[2]Fish! Philosophy, www.charthouse.com

The next focus of the FISH! Philosophy is to continually try to be present for the customer and totally attentive to what they are doing when they are doing it. In their training, the mongers use the phrase that "you need to be present for the customer like you are talking to your best friend." The implication about being present as it relates to schools is remarkably insightful. How often have we heard of students not being totally engaged in a lesson, or of a teacher being mentally or emotionally detached from the class? The FISH! Philosophy suggests that being present is a necessary component of successful interactions and educational theory would agree. I know a teacher who embodies this philosophy in every class. When she takes her daily attendance, she strives to make personal contact with each student, giving them the accurate impression that she is present for them and, in turn, asking them to be present for her. We need to be present and in the moment every time we work with a student, parent, or colleague. This idea is essential in a school for each student approach.

The third concept that the fishmongers live by is that each day we should set out to make a difference for others. It might come in the form of cheering up a customer, filling an order with quality products, or complimenting a person on their smile. The belief is that if we set out each day to make a difference, not only will we succeed, the effort will also increase our own feelings of fulfillment. Doesn't this concept resonate with the teacher in us? Isn't this why we went into teaching in the first place: to make a contribution? Beyond the obvious fit with the teaching profession, the idea of making a difference has huge implications for helping students become engaged, involved, and relevant.

The final principle of the FISH! Philosophy involves choosing our attitude. At the start of each day, we are presented with an opportunity to choose our attitude for the day. On most days, we clearly have a choice between negative and positive outcomes, and the folks at Pikes Place spur each other on to continually choose the positive. They theorize that excuse-making, blame, and feeling sorry for ourselves are self-inflicted conditions; we can choose to see the positive in most situations. What a wonderful way to come to school each day, expecting good things to happen instead of bad things.

On my best days, these philosophies create a great deal of self-satisfaction about my contribution to my family, students, school, and community. To laugh, to be present in the moment, to feel that I am making a difference, and to have control over my mood are powerful feelings. On my worst days, the habit of focusing on trying to accomplish these principles probably turns certain failure into possible success. I know without question that when I walk into a bank or a grocery store whose employees have received training in the Fish! Philosophy, it is obvious. Wouldn't it be grand if our students and their parents could see these four great philosophies at work in our schools?

Hope Flourishes

I would like to share a story that I found to be a great metaphor of why the quality of our work is so closely linked to hope. I received an e-mail several weeks ago from a proud mom who was relaying a positive experience she had with her son, a freshmen in high school. I read this lengthy communication with great interest as I always look for news that validates the great work my staff is doing. It has been said that ten of these positives correspondents are needed to offset one negative one, so I never pass up an opportunity to hear good news. Following is a summary of the story about a boy that I will call Bill.

Bill was part of a family of slim, nimble runners, but he had a wide body more suitable to football, a sport he did not enjoy. He frequently had to listen to lengthy conversations about running at the dinning room table. His older siblings were track stars, but Bill enjoyed baseball and basketball. Mom convinced Bill to go out for the cross-country team in the fall of his freshmen year in order to prepare for basketball and baseball. Bill agreed at first, but when the pre-season began, he was leaning toward just working out on his own. Mom convinced him to give the team a try as she believed his training would be more consistent and beneficial. He started working out with the team and seemed to really enjoy himself. The team was comprised of kids who treated each other with great respect and kindness and this atmosphere was reinforced by the coaches. He was the slowest on the team and often placed last in races, but eventually became very interested in his personal improvement.

After a month or so of practice, Bill's body began to change. He grew even more motivated to improve his time but because races are always run on different courses, it was hard for him to measure his improvement. His mom suggested that they go to the track and give him a time trial in the mile run. His personal best had been 9:48 prior to joining the team and his first attempt with Mom timing yielded an 8:22. Two weeks later, his older brother and some of his teammates came home from college and encouraged him to try the break the 8:00 barrier. He ran an 8:08.

After the cross-country season drew to a close, Bill asked Mom to time him one more time. As determined as he was to break eight minutes, he clocked in at 8:00.32. So close! Mom e-mailed the coaches and asked if they would consider having Bill try for his goal again with the other runners watching. They loved the idea and set a time and date for Bills one-mile challenge. Mom told Bill that she was going to be there to see him break his record.

On the day of the time trial, Mom got delayed at work and got to the track a few minutes late. As she approached the track, she heard the thunderous cheering of Bill's teammates as he came down the final stretch. Her eyes filled with tears when she saw that the kids were holding signs, beating drums, and yelling encouragement to Bill at the top of their lungs. Bill responded with strong, confident strides.

Bill crossed the line at 7:37 and was so emotionally lifted by the support of his team that he could have run another 7:37 right then. The future looks bright for the next generation when you gaze through Bill's eyes and the eyes of his mom.

I teared up as I read the e-mail and I did not know, until the very end, that Bill was not even one of my students. His mom had e-mailed this story to every school in our state that had a cross-country team. It did not matter that this was not about my staff or my students; it is a story of hope that all people can benefit from.

I have included it here because the themes of hope and support dovetail beautifully with my mission for this book. We can be beacons of hope for our students and support them in their daily quest to achieve their personal best.

Just like Bill's teammates, we can encourage and cheer our students and even our colleagues as we all journey toward great accomplishments.

Watch Out For The White Water

My one actual experience with white-water rafting left quite a lasting impression on me. I remember being nervous about the adventure as I was listening to the guide give his final instructions before we pushed off. The instructions were simple enough, with only five basic things to remember: all forward, all back, back left forward right, back right forward left, and hold on. Those were the directions for paddling and we were also told to remember to keep our toes out of the water and pointed downstream in the event we fall overboard. It all sounded simple enough. I jumped into the raft, confident that I could follow these instructions even though I was scared. I kept replaying these instructions in my head as we floated gently downstream on a mild sunny day. Soon, my nervousness subsided and I stopped focusing on the instructions and started to enjoy the beautiful scenery and the other people in the raft with me. When we came to some stronger currents, we had to use the skills the instructor had taught us. I remember thinking that this was fun and nowhere near as challenging as I had anticipated. We calmly responded to the guide's commands of all forward, all back, and so forth. All of this serenity evaporated as the raft proceeded around a bend in the river.

Suddenly, we hit white water and I sprang into panic mode. The skills that I had learned were long forgotten as the water kept rising and swirling faster by the second. The river was so loud that I could not hear the guide's instructions. As we went airborne over a place in the river called magic falls, I found myself holding on for dear life. I do not remember breathing, but must have been as I was screaming incoherently. The guide's simple instructions meant nothing to me now. I was in the middle of a raging river with protruding rocks flying by and I could have cared less when the guide said all forward; I was holding on! Of course, I lived to tell about my expedition down class-five rapids in northern Maine and frequently think back to those simple instructions I was given in the beginning.

You, too, have received some fairly straightforward instructions about how to position yourself for successful outcomes as you work to create a new mission for your work. You understand the significance of the interpersonal side of teaching and that the relationships you forge with students are what matters most. You have been given suggestions about being reflective about your work so that you are continually seeking to improve learning outcomes for your students. You have been encouraged to hold yourself to high standards of professionalism in the form of the twelve Rs. Hopefully, you have been convinced of the importance of working toward helping your students find relevance for themselves and to be given opportunities to practice democratic principles in a safe school setting. And finally, you have been exposed to some ideas that will help you to see the issues, questions, and concerns that affect education from a wider perspective. All of these appear doable until you return to the daily grind—until you hit white water.

I am certain that you will be challenged to remember all of this when the first crisis hits you at your school on Monday morning, but therein lies your biggest test. You can choose to forget that you have the means to take control of your work and join the many others who exist from day to day in mediocrity, or you can hold on to these principles and work to change the reality of your environment. You can accept the challenge and work your way up the continuum from novice to expert, or you can let the river get the best of you. The pathway to create a more personalized experience for your students is yours for the taking. Make no mistake; there will be challenges that come to test your meddle, but you have the tools within you that will allow you to soar above the rest.

If you are ready and willing, you can reconnect with why you became a teacher in the first place. You can make a huge impact at your school by helping students become successful learners while propelling yourself forward in a mode of continual improvement. Imagine what kind of changes would be possible if you and a simple majority of your fellow teachers could courageously adopt the ideas presented here? Think of what could happen in schools across America if we could get everyone to follow the tenets presented here? Before you close this book, consider making a commitment to the kind of teacher you want to be, and consider passing these ideas and ideals on to others.

Beginning today, and continuing to the day that you retire, you can choose to be a vital part of creating a school for each student, and to support them on their journey to personal greatness.

Chapter 6: Discussion Questions

1. The author indicated that schools are obsessed with keeping score. How does this go against the school for each student philosophy?
2. Discuss ways that intrinsic motivation could be developed in a school for each student setting. How does this differ from what occurs in a school for all students?
3. Generate a list of recent changes that have occurred in your school. How were these arrived at? Were any of these contextual? Could any be considered inspired?
4. How does the story about Bill's quest to improve his time in the mile run compare to ideas presented about schools becoming more personalized?
5. What barriers exist in your current situation that would hinder the adoption of a school for each student philosophy? What could be done to minimize or eliminate these barriers?
6. Consider a formal plan for moving your classroom or your school towards the school for each student model. What are some safe guards that could be implemented to handle the white water that you will encounter?

References and Readings

Beat of a Different Marcher. By Monte Selby and Debbie Silver. Rec. ©℗ 2002. Street Singer Music, BMI and Tato Tunes, ASCAP All rights reserved. Used by permission.

Bernard, Bonnie. *Resiliency: What we have Learned.* West Ed., 2004.

Bestor, Arthur. *Educational Wastelands: The Retreat from Learning in our Public Schools.* Quoted by David Kirp, Just Schools, supra. University of Illinois Press, 1953. p. 38.

Chaltain, Samuel. Executive director of the Five Freedoms Network, www.fivefreedoms. org

Collins, Jim. *Good to Great and the Social Sectors.* Harper Business, 2005.

Covey, Stephen R. *The 8th Habit.* Simon and Schuster, 2004.

DeZouche, Dorothy. Quote online www.faculty.ucc.edu/committee-pdc/quotes.htm

Dufour, Rick and Becky Dufour, www.solution-tree.com

Evans, Robert. *Family Matters: How Schools can Cope with the Crisis in Childrearing.* Jossey-Bass Publishers, 2004.

FISH! Philosophy, www.charthouse.com/content

Fullen, Michael, Peter Hall, and Carmel Crevola. *Breakthrough.* Corwin Press, 2006.

The Gates Foundation, www.gatesfoundation.org

Harvie, Keith. *Maine Educator* 66, no. 8 (April 2006). Used with permission.

Haberman, Martin. *Star Teachers of Children in Poverty* (1995). Kappa Delta Phi.

Herzberg, Fredrick, B. Mausner, and B. Bloch Snijdermen. *The Motivation to Work.* New York, 1959.

Kohn, Alfie. "The Risks of Rewards" *Teachers.net Gazette* 2, no. 4 (2001).

Jefferson, Thomas. Letter to William Charles Jarvis, 28 September 1820. *The Writings of Thomas Jefferson, Memorial Edition,* eds. Kipscomb and Bergh, 15:278.

Littky, Dennis and Samantha Grabelle. *The Big Picture: Education is Everyone's Business.* Association for Supervision and Curriculum Development, 2004.

Putnam, Robert D. *Bowling Alone: The Collapse and Revival of American Community.* Simon and Schuster, 2000.

National Association of Secondary School Principals. Printed with permission.

Quaglia, Russell. Quaglia Institute for Student Aspirations, www.qisa.org/about.php

Reeves, Douglas B., www.makingstandardswork.com

Ryan's Well Foundation, www.ryanswellfoundation.org

Saphier, Jon and Robert Gower. *The Skillful Teacher: Building your Teaching Skills.* Research for Better Teaching, Inc., 1979, www.rbteach.com

Schlechty, Philip. "On the Frontier of School Reform with Trailblazer, Pioneers and Settlers." *Journal of Staff Development* 14 (Fall 1993), 14:46–51.

Senge, Peter, Art Kleiner, Charlotte Roberts, Richard Ross, George Roth, and Bryan Smith. *The Dance of Change: The Challenges of Sustaining Momentum in Learning Organization.* Doubleday/Currency, 1999.

Siebert, Al. *The Resiliency Advantage: Master Change, Thrive under Pressure and Bounce Back from Setbacks.* Practical Psychology Press, 2005, www.resilencycenter.com

Stronge, James H. Qualities of Effective Teachers. Association for Supervision and Curriculum Development, 2002.

To Be and to Have. Philbert, Nicolas. Video. New York, 2004.

Waterman, Sheryn Spencer. *The Democratic Differentiated Classroom.* Eye on Education, 2007.

Whitaker, Todd, www.toddwhitaker.com